John Sullivan
Christmas 1978

HOW TO ASK FOR MORE AND GET IT

FRANCIS GREENBURGER
with
THOMAS KIERNAN

HOW TO ASK FOR MORE AND GET IT

The Art of Creative Negotiation

Doubleday & Company, Inc., Garden City, New York
1978

Library of Congress Cataloging in Publication Data

Greenburger, Francis
Kiernan, Thomas

    How to ask for more and get it: the art of creative negotiation
1. Title
ISBN 0-385-12495-3
Library of Congress Catalog Card Number 77–80889

For Laura, who has given me much,
including the inspiration and confidence
to complete this book.

Acknowledgments

I wish to acknowledge and thank several people who either directly or indirectly contributed to my ability to write this book.

Thank you, Father G., Leo F., Mother G., Esther W., Philip R., Sam P., Izzy A., Ken F., Michel Z., and George B.

F.G.

Authors' Note

This book is the result of a full collaboration between the authors. However, we have chosen to write it in the first-person voice of Francis Greenburger, since it is largely upon his knowledge and experience that the book is based.

F.G. AND T.K.

CONTENTS

Part Five
TACTICS

FOREWORD

Negotiation has been an integral part of my existence since I was a child. My father's profession (now mine) was largely dependent on his ability to negotiate favorable contracts for his clients. As an author's representative, or "literary agent," a primary function of his profession was to negotiate the terms of an author's contract with his publisher. Each deal is unique, and whether the stakes are as little as a $100 permission fee (as many of the contracts in our files are) or the $3 million one of my agent affiliates recently negotiated for a best-selling client, each contract represents an exchange which had to be arrived at by trading off the respective interests of each party, until a single set of goal compromises was agreed to.

Because of my father's influence, negotiation has always seemed a natural process to me. However, I have discovered that this is far from true for most people. After speaking with dozens of individuals, varying in background from a laboratory technician to the president of a multimillion-dollar service company, the greatest obstacle most people identify in negotiating for themselves is an irrational fear or embarrassment at the negotiating process. I urge you to confront this fear and to recognize that there is nothing wrong or improper in asking for your fair share.

Overcoming this fear, or not having it, has served me well. By using the concepts of negotiation described in this book, and having the willingness to assert them in my interest, I have managed in a relatively few years to amass substantial financial holdings.

At the tender age of sixteen, long before my father's death, I took my first steps toward building a real estate investment business which today owns and operates buildings with over a thousand Manhattan apartments. The literary agency, which my father left me when he died in 1971, depended on a select client list of fewer than fifty authors. Today the agency and its affiliates include more than twenty-five agents and employees, representing over four hundred authors, among them some of the most successful writers of our time.

Although my two business endeavors may seem worlds apart to you, they are actually very similar—each being totally dependent on the same basic skill, negotiating. Because I believe this to be a skill essential to every person's life, be they house person, business person, professional, or hippie, I have tried in this book to explain the negotiating process in such a way that it will be accessible to anyone who takes the time to read it. It is my hope that the few hours you invest in this book will be richly rewarding to you and improve your ability to get your fair share in business, in your professional life, and in your personal acquisitions and pursuits.

I wish you the best of success and luck in your endeavors.

FRANCIS GREENBURGER

HOW TO ASK FOR MORE AND GET IT

Part One
WHY NEGOTIATE

Chapter 1

The Need to Negotiate

Imagine yourself in any of the following situations:

You are about to walk into a realtor's office to make an offer on your dream house or to rent the apartment you've finally found after months of searching.

You are about to sit down with your spouse's lawyer to discuss the financial terms of your impending divorce.

Tomorrow you are to appear for your final interview with a company you feel sure will offer you the job you have been seeking, at which your salary and other benefits will be decided.

You have just met an attractive person at a party and would like to end the evening in bed with him or her.

You have just received a roofer's estimate for much-needed repairs to your house.

You are about to sit down with an auditor from the Internal Revenue Service (IRS).

Your bank has just offered you a mortgage for 60 per cent of the purchase price of the new house you dearly want to buy, but you need 80 per cent.

The foregoing are just a handful of the myriad transactions the average person faces during the course of his or her life. You can think of numerous corollaries in your own life, certainly. Some of these transactions are of an everyday nature and are relatively unimportant. Others, because they can affect one's career, one's relationships, one's lifestyle, one's well-being, or one's self-esteem, are of vital importance. Whether vital or incidental, all such experiences have two significant characteristics in common:

1. They anticipate an exchange, one in which something will be surrendered in order to gain something else.

2. They contain the probability of psychological and (usually) financial loss or gain.

These two characteristics constitute the dynamics of what is the single most frequent and important process of our interpersonal existence: *the exchange.*

To put it another way, all of us are confronted daily with countless exchanges, both ordinary and extraordinary, the outcomes of which largely define the quality of our lives. The "bottom line" of such exchanges is that we either gain or lose by them, financially and otherwise. Motivated by our innate self-interest, we naturally hope to acquire more than we give away. More often than not, however, we end up losing more than we gain. Why? Because we do not know *how to negotiate* our needs, our rights, our hopes, and our wishes.

Life is many things, poetic and prosaic. What it is, above all, is an endless series of exchanges between people, one thing for another. The common instrumentality of all such exchanges is *negotiation*. Negotiation, whether direct or indirect, is the fundamental leavening agent of human life.

We all relentlessly seek to obtain more for ourselves (or for those we represent). We seek to improve our positions with respect to our immediate peers and with respect to the larger circle of our society. This impulse is as deeply ingrained in us as the instinct to avoid pain. Yet the gap between our drive to better our positions and our ability to fulfill that drive is, for many of us, vast. This is due in large measure to the fact that most of us are unskilled and unschooled in the art and craft of negotiation.

How to Ask for More and Get It is not, as the title might suggest, a book for the greedy, pursuing compulsive and unrealistic dreams of acquiring more worldly wealth. Rather, it is designed to help the average person get his due in the thousands of exchanges, both mundane and important, that punctuate his or her life.

The book proceeds from two certifiable premises. One is that most people are unskilled in, and often embarrassed by, the act of negotiating on their own behalf. The second is that most people, when required to deal in significant transactions, are too easily intimidated—either by the nature and scope of the transaction itself or by those on the other side of the transaction, or both—into giving up more than they get. This is especially true when the exchange concerns matters about which the opposite party is presumed to have more knowledge, expertise, legal power, or financial assets.

Be it the employee bargaining for a raise, the tenant applying for a lease, the homeowner planning an expansion, the spouse settling a quarrel, the businessman seeking financing, the sick person needing medical attention, or the car owner requiring urgent repairs—all have in common the fact that an exchange, on an agreed-upon basis, will take place. Who will get what and how much, and what and how much will have to be yielded in return, are solely dependent on each individual's ability to recognize and advance his needs, interests, and desires.

Should the prospective tenant stoically accept the rent increase and sign the standard lease the landlord shoves in front of him? Or should he try to argue for better terms?

Should the prospective client docilely yield to the lawyer's demand for a high retainer? Or should he try to obtain a lower fee?

Should the homeowner quietly agree to the contractor's estimate, even when it is accompanied by a mournful tale of spiraling labor and lumber costs? Or should he commiserate with the man and then quietly suggest that he refigure his estimate downward?

Should the spouse anxious to end the marriage guiltily concur in the other party's financial demands? Or should he or she pragmatically hold out for more realistic terms?

These are but a few of the many examples of important exchanges which I hope to show you how to approach and consummate to your best advantage. The key will be the art and craft of negotiation.

Unfortunately, negotiation is a subject that is not taught in the schools most people attend. Not even the most legendary negotiators of our times acquired their bargaining acumen in the classroom. One might therefore conclude that the negotiator's skill is a gift—some have it, most don't. Not true. The fact that some people are naturally gifted negotiators does not preclude the more important fact that the skill can easily be acquired. Everyone has the potential to be an effective negotiator.

To fulfill that potential demands four things. *First*, motivation—that is, recognition on the part of those who envy it in others that negotiating skill can become an eminently practical and beneficial component of their own lives. That it will save them money, assure them of increased material benefits, and provide them with greater psychological freedom.

Second, the realization that any exchange is a two-way affair and that the opposite party is in a similar position as oneself. In other words, one must learn to understand that the opposite party in any exchange never possesses superior power or position. This is because what one is trading is the equalizer.

Third, insight into the dynamics of all of life's important exchanges, followed by an expanding knowledge of the techniques needed to master these dynamics.

Fourth, practice. Practice not only sharpens skills; it also overcomes most people's natural reluctance to ask for more than they think they can get and instills the self-confidence to ask for even more than that!

It is axiomatic in the world of experienced negotiators that most people pathetically underestimate their own power to bargain for a more equitable exchange, that they will usually accept exactly or approximately what has been offered to them. The idea that the person making the offer may be more than willing to consummate the exchange at a lower yield or on an entirely different basis seldom occurs to most people on the other side of the transaction. They simply assume that they must accept what has been proffered or else decline; they rarely suspect that a third alternative, no matter how much more desirable it may be to them, either exists or is possible.

Through this book it is hoped that this misconception can be forever erased. I hope to give you a new and invaluable skill which will permit you to get your fair share from every exchange you enter into, so that you need never again be intimidated or shortchanged. Permit me to introduce you to the world of effective negotiation, and I promise you a new share of the world.

Part Two

CRITERIA, RATIONALES, AND COUNTERRATIONALES

Chapter 2

Beginning

In golf you may be capable of consistently driving the ball, straight as a die, two hundred yards or more. This suggests great technical proficiency. But if you don't have a strategic sense of where to aim your drives, when to sacrifice distance for accuracy, how to try to position yourself for a good second shot, your power and proficiency are just as likely to get you in trouble as not.

A negotiated exchange, like any game, also has a strategic direction. To maximize the effectiveness of your "shots" it is important to advance them in a tactical order.

The direction of a negotiation will usually proceed through three basic stages that are set not by the opponents but by the very nature of the negotiating process. The first is the stage in which the opponents establish their *criteria*, set out their *goals* (take an opening position), and explain the *rationales* behind their goals.

The second stage consists of trying to fulfill information goals and establishing common ground.

The third stage consists of reaching for primary and secondary goal concessions that will provide momentum and bring about compromise.

Each of these stages can themselves be used tactically within the negotiation. The more specialized tactics are merely tools to be used to expedite the completion of each of the three basic tactical stages.

Explaining Your Criteria

Prior to entering into any exchange, one should establish a set of criteria for the goals to be achieved in the exchange. Your criteria give your opponent the first hint of what some of your goals are. Likewise, your opponent's criteria give you the first hint of what his or her goals will be. Establishing your criteria, then, is the first important tactical stage of a negotiated exchange.

Criteria can take many forms. They can materialize in an advertisement you place seeking an exchange. They can be contained in as simple a verbal statement as "Would you be interested in investing in my business?" They are "invitations" or offers to consider an exchange. In other words, your criteria for an exchange will usually, wholly or partially, be stated in some form as to attract or interest a second party with whom you wish to consummate the exchange.

However, criteria serve a second and even more critical tactical purpose. They enable you to put together a set of values and goals that provide a realistic opening position in the negotiation. Since your first significant tactical move in a negotiation is stating your opening position, before doing so you should organize your criteria as tightly and thoroughly as you can so that your position will have as much thrust and sustained power as possible. With your criteria well organized and your opening position a strong one, your opponent may well be persuaded to counter with a less resolute position of his own than he or she otherwise would.

The following is an example of the criteria I established when I recently decided to hire an architect for an urban renewal project I was involved in:

1. The architect needs to have experience in urban residential renewal work.

2. He should be young, but with at least seven years of general architectural experience.

3. He must be willing to work at an hourly rate of not more than $25 and must be willing to set a maximum hourly rate estimate for each job. (Many architects prefer to set their fees as a percentage of total construction costs or are unwilling to set hourly maximums.)

4. He must be someone who understands and is sympathetic to the type of work I want to do. He should be a man I like and with whom I will feel comfortable working.

After establishing these criteria, I set up interviews with several architects who had been recommended to me by various sources as potentially qualified. I met with each and, explaining my criteria and the rationales behind them, alerted them to my needs. In the process of doing this, I was establishing my opening position and at the same time setting up information goals the achievement of which would tell me to what extent each prospect was willing and able to fulfill my criteria.

In response, each architect described his background and experience, his interest in urban rehabilitation work, his billing practices, and so on. In effect, they were responding with their criteria and the rationales for them. I was able to get a personal sense of each of them and determine how well I thought each would be able to work with me.

By exchanging criteria in the way that we did, the architects and I were further able to decide whether there was a basis for negotiating a contract. At the beginning of any negotiation, the exchange of criteria is crucial because it not only sets the tone for the rest of the negotiation, but it also in many cases determines whether—in view of the disparity between goal objectives—a negotiation is possible. It is always important, therefore, to use the tactic of criteria-establishment judiciously. By stating your criteria you are outlining your principal goals. No matter how convincingly you furnish them with persuasive rationales, you always run the risk of having the negotiation aborted at the outset if you appear too rigid in your criteria. Tactic, technique, style —these are the things you should be aware of when establishing your criteria and taking your opening position. Your opening position should never be self-defeating, except when you want it to be. (This might occur when you determine that you don't want to negotiate with a particular person, and the most convenient way to abort the negotiation is to put forth self-defeating criteria.)

Criteria-establishment fulfills another valuable tactical function besides defining the potential for negotiation. In explaining your criteria you will usually provide your opponents with rationales for them. "I am asking $30,000 per year beginning salary because I don't feel that it would be worth my while to change jobs for less," is an example of a criterion or goal rationale. It is often possible to convert criteria into separate negotiating rationales. By becoming rationales, criteria then assume a secondary tactical function.

The process works this way. When you establish and explain your criteria at the beginning of a negotiation, they gain an "historical perspective" later on in the proceedings. When important goals remain unsettled later on in the negotiation, you can reinforce your position by pointing to the early criteria linked to these goals.

For instance, later in my negotiation with the architect I hope to hire, I will be able to say, in supporting my still-unagreed-upon $25-an-hour fee goal, "As you'll recall, one of the criteria I established when we first met was the fact that I could not pay more than $25 an hour."

Here I have converted one of my criteria into a tactical rationale. I may have no other precedent to justify my $25-an-hour goal. I cannot show that such a fee concept is customary, nor can I point out cases of other architects' engaging in such work at such fees. All I have is my original criterion, converted into a tactical rationale, to persuade the architect to agree. Because the architect consented to enter into a negotiation with me based on our first interview, during which I explained my criteria, he is now obliged to negotiate using the $25 figure as a basic frame of reference.

The architect may well have indicated to me, in the initial expression of his criteria, that he usually gets $60 per hour. But the fact that he pursued the negotiation in the face of my $25-an-hour statement is an implicit indication that a fee in the $25-to-$60 range is possible. Presumably, it would be much closer to $25, since I described this as "maximum" in my criteria explanation while he described his $60 as "usual."

Criteria are things which we constantly establish in our minds when we are confronted by exchanges. Criteria are the "policy" of exchanges. When you decide to go to a casual, medium-priced French restaurant, you have in fact established your criteria for a particular meal exchange. When you decide to buy a house, information you give to the broker about the neighborhood, number of rooms, architectural style, age of the house, and price range constitutes your criteria. The advertisement which announces a job opening for a bank trainee—no experience necessary and $9,500 per year to start—is the bank's statement of its criteria for the job.

Often in negotiating you will find that you have to revise or otherwise alter your criteria as "informational goals" are achieved. When you do, you should always be sure that your new criteria do not place you in a position that will render the exchange unfavorable to you.

As an example, let's say that you establish various criteria for the house you want to buy, including a maximum price of $85,000. After researching the market with several brokers, you become convinced that the house you want is not available for less than $125,000. Do you raise your price criterion upward?—only after carefully considering whether the increased price is within your long-term financial means.

Negotiating cannot make the impossible possible. What it does is make the possible probable. Always establish your exchange criteria realistically. If you have champagne tastes but only a beer income, do not try to corner the market on champagne. Instead, seek out and get the best beer you can.

Don't let fashions, envy, greed, or lust dictate your criteria, as they may ensnare you in uneconomic and unworkable situations which will eventually result in your losing much more than you gain. Criteria are at once the introduction to and foundation of all successful negotiations. If you establish them thoughtfully and realistically, they will be invaluable in consistently guiding you to beneficial exchange positions.

Taking a Position

The second tactical aspect of the first stage of a negotiation is the taking of positions, or the making of offers or proposals. This is all part of the ritual dynamics of negotiation.

In tennis, a game cannot be considered under way until someone first serves. In negotiation, the declaration of one or the other party's opening position is equivalent, tactically, to the first serve in a tennis match. If it is you who are taking the position, you want to be sure that you don't double-fault.

In the course of simple exchanges it is almost always the "seller"—that is, the individual or organization *from whom* the other party is seeking something—who has established his or her criteria and takes the first position. This is the conventional ritual of the exchange process. For example, if you want to buy a bottle of shampoo, you are expected to go into a store and pay whatever the price marked on the bottle says you should pay. If you respond to an advertisement, you are expected, at least theoretically, to agree to whatever criteria and terms are stated. If you are offered a raise, you are expected to accept it and ask for no more. If your boy friend offers to marry you, you are expected to say "Yes" or "No," but are not expected to debate the terms of the proposal.

One of the things your new "how-to-ask-for-more-and-get-it" approach to life will help you do is to reverse this ritual. That is, in any exchange, the important terms should be negotiated, not predetermined. Your philosophy should be: "I will consider entering this exchange with you . . . if!" And then, "This is my offer."

In more complex or less clear-cut exchanges, of course, it is not always the "seller" who serves first. On other occasions, although you may be the "seller"—that is, potentially in control of the opening position—it may be to your tactical advantage, psychologically or otherwise, to force your opponent to state his or her position first.

Back in co-author Thomas Kiernan's days as a football coach, whenever his team won the flip of the coin, he would often instruct his team captain to choose to kick off rather

than receive. Sometimes he did this for psychological reasons—to so impress his opponents of his own team's
confidence in themselves, whether it was real or not, that
they would begin the game already demoralized. Other
times he did it because by kicking off he would be favored
by wind or sun factors when he got the ball. It was always a
tactic. Naturally, if his kick-off man made a feeble kick,
much of the tactic's value would have been compromised by
technical deficiency.

The opening position or offer in a negotiation will detail
the maximum primary goal expectations of the party making
the offer. (It need not, however, reveal all one's primary
goals. It is sometimes better to withhold a primary goal,
which an opponent may not recognize as such, for later discussion. It may then be possible to introduce it as a secondary goal which the opponent will be less inclined to resist.)
It will reflect the range explicitly or implicitly suggested by
the party's established criteria. And it will usually be intended to invite the other party to declare his or her opening position or to make a counteroffer.

I call up Bill Lewis, the architect I have settled on as
the most desirable prospect in my search. He already knows
my criteria from our previous meeting. I am now ready to
make him an offer.

I tell Lewis that I would like to use him on a specific
building-rehabilitation job and that if it works out to my sat-
isfaction, I will certainly use him on additional jobs. I offer
him $25 an hour and tell him that I feel the job should carry
a hundred-hour maximum, which means that he stands to
earn, at most, $2,500.

What I have not revealed to him is one of my primary
goals: that the job be completed in five days, or sixty hours.
(I figure that he will be putting twelve hours a day into the
job.)

Lewis now takes his position. He would like to work

for me, he says, but his payroll and office overhead demands that he get $60 an hour (this is his rationale). In view of the fact that I might use him in the future, he is willing to cut his fee to $45 an hour (which means, on my hundred-hour estimate, he would stand to earn $4,500 instead of $2,500).

I counter with some further rationales of my own, including the criterion-turned-rationale of my original $25 as the basis of our first discussion and ask him if he would further reduce his fee to $40 an hour. If he would, I would then come up from my $25.

Lewis, because he obviously wants the job for its longer-term potential, agrees. Okay, I say, I will pay you $40 an hour. That's quite a concession. In view of my willingness to concede on the fee question, I must revise my thinking on the time factor. For that money, I expect Lewis to work a little harder. So I tell him that I want him to agree that he'll finish the job in five days, or sixty hours of work. I'll give an extra five-hour cushion to sixty-five hours.

Lewis agrees, although he stands to make $100 less at his $40 fee than he would have at $25, according to the way I structured my original offer. His primary goal was to get the highest fee he could, and his secondary goal was to ensure the likelihood of further work at that minimum fee, which he would then try to negotiate higher.

My primary goals were to meet my $2,500 budget for architectural services and to get the job done in five days. I reached both my goals. I did so by making it appear in my opening position that my primary concern was the amount of the fee and not the total architectural cost of the job. I made a secondary goal seem primary, while holding back my real primary goal until my opponent's primary goal was fulfilled.

The way in which a position is described can often be the difference between night and day. I recently read about the Russian press account of a track meet between an American and a Russian, in which the American had won. The Russians reported the event by saying "that the Russian contender had come in second, and the American, next to last."

When taking your opening position or making your opening offer, you should always structure it in the most tactically advantageous way you can. As you gain experience in "asking for more," you will develop an increasingly polished sense for the niceties of position taking and its tactical dynamics.

There is nothing immoral, dishonest, or unethical about this. It is simply the best way to play a very competitive game. It is a game in which, if you fail to use all the tactics and techniques available to you, you will continue to yield to someone else what is rightfully yours.

I recently attended a funeral mass for a friend at a local church. Smack in the middle of the mass, with my friend's casket barely closed and his family struggling to control their tears, everything stopped while a collection was taken up. Not for the family, but for the church. Somehow I thought that that was inappropriate. But I guess I was alone in my thinking. Everyone else present momentarily forgot their tears and their sadness to dig into purses and wallets for contributions to the collection basket. Evidently it was accepted practice for the church to ask for its just due, no matter the circumstances.

Rationales

Each criterion, each goal you reveal in a negotiation should be accompanied by a rationale. Offering rationales is a tactic that turns your problems, your interests, your hopes into your opponent's. Rationales give your goals integrity and dimension in your opponent's eyes. They force your opponent to take your goals seriously and can be very effec-

tive, if properly phrased and timed, in gaining goal concessions.

In many of the negotiating anecdotes I will recount
throughout this book, I will include examples of the rationale tactic without pointing them out. A "rationale" is
simple to define: it is your explanation to your opponent of
why you feel a particular goal is justified.

In explaining my criteria to Bill Lewis and the other
architects I interviewed, I spent fifteen minutes talking
about the housing shortage in New York and the collapse of
the real estate industry. I told them that I thought the
rehabiliation of condemned buildings was the answer and
that I had developed an economic formula on which to base
it. I explained that it required keeping things to the basics
and fighting excess costs everywhere. It required using
materials that were inexpensive but good values, labor that
was skilled but willing to work at lower than standard rates.

I added that the architects too would be required to adjust their fees to fit into my formula so that my plan could
work. I wished I could pay more, I said, but it wasn't possible. However, by agreeing to work on my terms, they would
be helping me to create work for the unemployed, solve the
housing shortage and revive the real estate industry, which
would mean more work for them in the future.

In explaining my need for a maximum on billable hours
vis-à-vis their services, I pointed out that one of the greatest
problems in construction was cost overruns. My ability to
attract the financing that would support my plan depended
on accuracy and reliability in budgeting my construction-
rehabilitation projects. I was required to place cost ceilings
on all aspects of the projects—an essential control to ensure
that my budgets were not overrun.

What was I really doing in presenting these rationales?
I was saying, "Look, I've got work for you that no one else

has. If you want this job and want further work from me in the future, you have to guarantee my success. My problem is your problem. This is the way I have to go about it, and if you want to work with me, this is what you have to do. If it succeeds, we'll all come out ahead."

I created reasons—rationales—why each of the architects should concede to my goals, and how doing so would benefit them. My rationales were logical, candid, and credible. They were also honest and true, although I will agree that they reflected primarily my own subjective view of reality and were designed principally to advance my own interests.

Rationales are not just important persuasion tactics. In many ways they are the lifeblood of a negotiation; they provide continuing communication and information, the very elements without which a negotiation would die, let alone be born.

Counterrationales

Counterrationales are exactly what the phrase suggests: rationales designed to counter or offset those of an opponent. They have most of the same qualities of rationales and are no less important as a tactic.

Whenever you receive a rationale from an opponent to support one of his or her goal objectives, you should recognize it for what it is and be prepared to counter it with one of your own. The more powerful your counterrationale, the more likely your opponent will be tempted to revise his and thus modify his criteria and goals.

A counterrationale has three basic functions, which are, in order of ascending importance, as follows:

1. At the least, it should explain to your opponent why you cannot accept the goal objective that underlies his rationale.

2. It should explain, when possible, why that goal objective may actually be contrary to his best interests.

3. When possible, it should refute his rationale and its underlying goal as erroneous or inconsistent and should prove why it is so.

Let me give an example of how counterrationales should work, using myself as, so to speak, the victim. This was another occasion when I was negotiating to hire an architect's services. I used many of the same budgetary rationales that I had employed with the architects of my earlier anecdote. This time, however, I was up against an architect, John Mason, who happened to be a very sharp negotiator as well.

At our second meeting Mason responded to my limitation on billable hours—in this case, I had set a maximum of 125 hours for his work—by saying that, based on his considerable experience, my estimate of what it would take to properly complete the job was "overly optimistic." He explained that while it was conceivably possible to do the design work in 125 hours, this would leave no time for him to perform two other parts of the job that would be of considerable benefit to me.

The first was this: he wanted to do an alternate research study on materials for the job in question, which might result in a 10 per cent saving on my total construction costs.

Second, he wanted to be able to make frequent on-site inspections to be sure that the job was being executed properly. These inspections would be necessary to ensure that the other cost-saving techniques Mason intended to incorporate in his plans were properly understood by the subcontractors.

By the use of these counterrationales, Mason clearly

showed why he would have difficulty in accepting my goal that he spend no more than 125 hours on the project. He linked a more favorable goal concession on my part to my self-interest—that is, my primary goal of minimizing costs. And to a certain degree, although in a most amicable way, he discredited my time estimate by pointing out that it did not take into account two vital areas of his work—areas that could further reduce my costs.

I had also wanted Mason to take on the job at a markedly lower hourly fee than he was accustomed to. He told me that while he was prepared to work at a low minimum rate on my rehabilitation jobs, he was reluctant to have that rate expressed in an exact hourly figure, or at least in one that was so low. If the figure became public knowledge, it would be difficult to explain to his other clients, who paid him more and in a sense made it possible for him occasionally to take on jobs such as mine in which his profit margin was next to nothing.

Again, Mason gave me a compelling reason for his inability to concede to my goal of a $25-an-hour fee. Eventually we agreed on an entirely different fee arrangement than I had originally conceived. If Mason had proposed it in our first meeting as a criterion and goal, I would have been reluctant to even consider it. But his well-timed tactical use of convincing counterrationales led me to different goal ranges than I had envisioned, yet one that remained responsive to my criteria.

We ultimately agreed on a base fee of $3,750. It was expressed in our contract as a fixed amount. No hourly figure was given, but the amount was equivalent of 150 hours at $25. In addition, I agreed to give him a bonus of 25 per cent of any savings he produced on my originally budgeted $75,000 construction costs. If Mason could reduce the costs as much as he said he could, he stood to increase his unexpressed hourly fee by almost 50 per cent.

Shaping the Negotiation

Rationales and counterrationales are the ebb and flow of negotiation. They define goal objectives, indicate areas of goal compromise, create the basis of goal agreements, and occasionally create new goals as the negotiation proceeds. They also help to satisfy information goals and lead to the establishment of common ground.

As the ebb and flow develops, it imposes a certain tactical shape on the progress of the negotiation. Every negotiation takes its original shape from the traditional rituals and customs of negotiation. But as the interactions of criteria, positioning, rationales, and counterrationales superimpose themselves upon the original shape, the shape will change, developing its own unique strategic direction.

The traditional negotiation begins with a consideration of the obvious or implicitly acknowledged primary goals. It will gradually proceed to secondary goals, more or less in the order of their importance. Secondary goals will be called on earlier than their priorities might at first indicate when you discover that a mix or linkage of primary and secondary goals will elicit a set of interrelated goal concessions or agreements from your opponent. Goals on which agreement cannot be immediately reached will be postponed and reconsidered later in the negotiation. Primary goals of yours which your opponent is not yet aware of (because you choose to conceal them) will remain unrevealed until later in the negotiation and will be introduced as secondary goals, so that counterbalancing primary goal concessions will not be required of you in reaching agreement on the disguised primary goal.

As the negotiation gains further shape, prior goal agreements may be adjusted to counterbalance favorable or unfavorable compromises on subsequent goal agreements. The negotiation will be complete when concessions, compromises, and agreements have been established for each of the respective party's goal objectives. The terms of the exchange having been determined, the exchange is ratified and completed in an agreed-upon manner.

Perhaps the process and tactical shape of a negotiation can be summarized more clearly in this way:

1. Exchange of criteria.

2. Opening position.

3. Consideration of primary goals (except withheld ones).

4. Consideration of secondary goals which can be linked to primary-goal agreements.

5. Consideration of unresolved secondary goals.

6. Introduction of *withheld* primary goals as secondary ones.

7. Resolution of primary and/or secondary goals on which agreement could not be made earlier.

8. The total agreement: agreements reached on all goal objectives.

9. The exchange is made.

Part Three
GOALS

Chapter 3

Your Goals: Knowing What You Want

There are no shortcuts to success in any of life's endeavors. History has taught us that success results from a compound of drive, ability, and hard work, laced with a modicum of luck. These components may operate in varying proportions between one individual and the next, but you can be sure that no one achieves success unless all four are functioning.

Success in negotiation—in asking for more and getting it—requires no less. This book, although it can function as an essential aid, is in no sense a magic path to your success in getting more. I intend to set you on the road to successful negotiation, but the degree to which you eventually *are* successful depends on the extent to which you pursue that path, how resolute you are in applying the concept of negotiation to your daily life, and how lucky and perceptive you are in exploiting the various parameters of each exchange you engage in.

Skills can only be developed through work and practice

—through negotiation itself. Before you undertake to begin
such practice, however, you should acquaint yourself with
certain fundamental facts that will enable you to prepare
properly for any negotiation. So far, I have discussed a number of abstract basic principles, which should give you an
overview of the dynamics of the exchange process. Now you
are ready to face the more concrete fundamentals of effectively negotiating most of your exchanges. In this and the
next three chapters, I will outline these fundamentals.

Knowing What You Want

You have just decided to buy a used car and have determined that you want to spend no more than $2,000 for it.
If you are like most people, the first thing you would do is to
turn to the used-car classifieds of your local newspaper to
see what is selling in the $1,500–$2,000 range. This would
give you an idea of what you might expect to get for $2,000.
If you were interested in more exact information, you might
pick up one of those used-car price guides that tell you the
market or "book" value of particular years and makes of
used cars.

With this information in hand, you might decide that a
mint-condition, well-equipped, two-year-old Chevy or Ford
is the car most suited to your price limitations and needs.
You would then go back to the classified section and scan
the ads for such cars. Or you would make the rounds of your
local used-car dealers. Or both.

After a couple of days of looking at two-year-old
Chevys and Fords, you will have learned several things: (1)
that most of the mint-condition cars you have seen are being
offered for considerably more than your $2,000 limit; (2)
that the only two-year-old cars being offered at $2,000 are
those that are in markedly less than top condition; (3) that

the only mint-condition cars you have seen at $2,000 are three-year-old models.

What you have done to this point is to research and establish your goal objectives for a contemplated exchange—the purchase of a car. These goal objectives will serve you in the same way driving directions do to arrive at a specified location: they detail the landmarks and goals of the upcoming exchange.

The use of goals, however, is a bit more complex than it might superficially appear. In a nonnegotiated exchange, goals are one-dimensional—the exchange is simply the trading of one goal for another. To get the car you want, you must either pay more than $2,000 or else accept a three-year-old model rather than the two-year-old car you wanted. In a negotiated exchange, however, goals become an integral part of the negotiation. They cause the negotiation to progress on different levels and thus are multidimensional.

The effective negotiator will invariably use his goals to shape his strategy and tactics and will manipulate his goals (and his opponent's) to materially influence the outcome of the exchange. In striving to achieve the goal of a top-condition, particular-model-year car at a given price, the skilled negotiator will seek to identify other goal areas which will appear as a compromise to his opponent but are in fact not essential to him (car color, mileage, etc.). Hence goals—their establishment and use—are probably the most important components of the negotiating process. In preparing to negotiate, it is absolutely imperative that you establish a hierarchy of goals which you can then manipulate and integrate with various tactics and techniques as the negotiation progresses.

Types of Goals

When you decided to buy a good used car, you were seeking the fulfillment of a number of goals, although you might not have been aware of it.

Let's say that your need of a reliable car to get you to work each day is your primary reason for deciding to scrap your current car, which has become troublesome. In checking your budget, the maximum amount of money you have available to buy a car is $2,000. I will call these *primary*, or *essential, goals.*

But there are other factors that have to be considered, including your preferences in color, body style, interior and so on. Although you hope to acquire a car that looks as good as it runs, these factors are not imperative. For you, they comprise your *secondary*, or *nonessential, goals.*

You also hope to take delivery of the car you buy within a week, since your current heap may prove totally nonfunctional at any moment. This is what I call a *short-term goal.*

You will also probably have a *long-term goal*—that the car should be durable and last for a number of years to come.

In searching for the car you want, you will have two further categories of goals in mind. One is what I will call your *informational goal*. This, simply, is your attempt to find out the true mechanical condition of the car you select before you actually buy it. Ideally, you would like the car checked over by an independent mechanic.

The other is what I will call your *warranty goals.* Whenever you enter into an exchange, you want to be sure that the opposite party and the thing he or she is offering are in fact as represented. If someone is offering an object, or cash, or some less tangible item such as a commitment, you want to be sure (1) that the party has the legal right to offer the item, and (2) that the item will perform as represented.

Car manufacturers, appliance manufacturers, building contractors, and others generally advertise the fact that they will guarantee (or give a warranty) that their products or services are free of any defects or breakdowns for a specified period or they will replace or repair parts in question free of charge.

In many of life's exchanges, however, there is not even an implicit warranty. It is simply a matter of *Caveat emptor,* or "Let the buyer beware." Therefore, your warranty goals should be an integral part of any negotiation.

All of these goals are basic components of any negotiated exchange. Each goal to varying degrees—depending on the type and nature of the exchange—plays a vital role in your participation in an exchange, although in perfunctory exchanges you might not be consciously aware of them.

In preparing to negotiate an exchange, however, you *should* become keenly aware of them. To establish and understand your various goals are key factors in preparing to negotiate. How to use your knowledge of your goals is a skill I will discuss in detail when I get to the negotiation itself. It is sufficient for now for you to review the types of goals you must concern yourself with when you prepare to negotiate. They are:

Your Primary Goals
Your Secondary Goals
Your Short-Term Goals
Your Long-Term Goals
Your Informational Goals
Your Warranty Goals

It is important also to remember that these six goal categories do not function each in their own pigeonholes, but usually interface and interact with one another. In other words, although a primary goal in wanting to buy a car may stem from an immediate need for transportation, one does not go out and buy the first thing on four wheels that one sees. Other goals enter the picture, several of them often carrying equal weight in the final decision about what car to buy. It is the extent of one's skill in balancing this goal interaction that is generally the measure of an effective negotiator.

Chapter 4

Knowing What Your Opponent Wants

But it is not just one's own goals that an effective negotiator must balance. Equally important in preparing for a successful negotiation is a solid understanding of your opponent's goals.

In a take-it-or-leave-it exchange you would pay no attention to the opposite party's goals. But in a negotiated exchange in which you are attempting to get more than you would ordinarily be given, your awareness of your opponent's goals is crucial to your success.

I recall an occasion when, as a literary agent, I was representing a woman who had just written a book and who needed to acquire a large number of photographs from a news agency to illustrate it. The woman, whom I shall call Pamela, had contracted with a publisher to write the book on a relatively low expense budget, one that allowed her to pay at most only $10 per picture, whereas all the news agencies charged a standard $50 per photo. She had made the rounds of the news agencies and had gotten nowhere in her efforts to negotiate a lower fee scale. However, a salesman at one agency invited her back to talk further. She asked me to go with her and help her try to reach an accommodation that she could afford.

Pamela and I arrived at the agency at the appointed hour and were shown to the office of the sales manager, along with the salesman Pamela had spoken to originally. She explained her financial limitations and gave them a list of the photos she needed. She then made her "pitch," suggesting that they agree to an arrangement in which she would pay $10 per photo in advance, with the agency to receive a share in the royalties in her book once it was published.

I knew that Pamela was unlikely to succeed in this, but I had suggested she use it as an opening gambit simply to get a process of communicating going and at the same time to open up to our inspection the agency's goals. (The salesman would not have involved his boss unless the agency was genuinely interested in finding a way to make a deal on the photos.)

As I expected, the sales manager politely rejected Pamela's proposal as being too speculative. He had been with the organization for thirty years, he said. He described at length and with great pride how the agency had developed and declared that if it had had to depend for its growth on speculative ventures such as the one Pamela proposed, it would never have reached its present state of prosperity—a prosperity that permitted it to serve the publishing industry with distinction.

It soon became clear to me that what was at stake in this meeting was not money (among other things, I had learned earlier, the news agency was nonprofit), but that the sales manager's primary goal was a psychological one. This man's main ambition was to gain recognition for what he and the agency had built up over the course of thirty years. I asked a few questions designed to elicit further information about the agency's accomplishments and reputation in the publishing world. To each I got a lengthy and detailed response from the sales chief, who was brimming with pride and a sense of self-importance. I found it all genuinely fascinating and complimented the man on his achievements.

After half an hour of this, I gradually eased the conversation back to the matter at hand. Picking up the thread of his distrust of the speculative nature of royalties, I told the sales manager that, in the light of what he had been saying, I agreed completely that a royalty arrangement would be out of character for his agency. I proposed as an alternative a system of conditional deferred payments on Pamela's part (in essence, the same arrangement Pamela had suggested, but structured in a way to make it seem less uncertain). An "iron-clad contract" would detail these payments, I said. In the meantime, the agency would have played a role in the publication of an important book, and if the book received the attention everyone expected it to, the agency's name and reputation would be further enhanced through the photo credits. I am happy to say that we wrapped up the meeting with a verbal agreement, to be ratified by a contract the next day, that gave Pamela everything she had wanted and more.

I recount this negotiating experience to illustrate the importance of being constantly sensitive to your opponent's goals. Had I at the beginning of our meeting tried to put forward my financial proposal, the sales manager would never have agreed. Instead, I used the beginning stages of the negotiation to allow my opponent to reveal himself. As it turned out, I discovered that his primary goals were what to another might have been secondary or long-term goals. That is, his main concern was to elicit respect for himself and his agency, and only secondarily was he bent on ensuring that the $50 rate would be paid.

I have left out several technical details of the foregoing

negotiation because I am not yet ready to get into specific techniques and tactics. The lesson to be learned here is that the first element of negotiating skill is not some magic and exotic mix of fast talk and glibness. Rather, it is a careful, perceptive, informed, and well-reasoned approach to the determining what is really at stake in the exchange. The fundamentals are not just the items being exchanged, but the goals of the respective parties to the exchange, which may encompass much that is not obvious or material. Perhaps the greatest hurdle you must leap in transforming yourself from passive acceptor to active negotiator is the recognition and application of the fact that because people have a variety of goals or priorities when executing an exchange, they are inevitably flexible in what they want. Often, what they really want most is not always what at first blush they may *seem* to want most. By being sensitive to the role that goals play in shaping an exchange, you can often get more than what you originally expect. This is as true with regard to people who enter exchanges from positions of power as it is to those who enter them from positions of weakness.

The different types of goals that I listed as ones which we should identify for ourselves are equally applicable to our opponents:

Opponent's Primary Goals
Opponent's Secondary Goals
Opponent's Short-Term Goals
Opponent's Long-Term Goals
Opponent's Informational Goals
Opponent's Warranty Goals

Eventually, the concept of goals becomes second nature to the skilled negotiator, and by breaking down and identifying your own, you will reinforce your ability to recognize and define your opponent's.

Chapter 5

Goal Management

The identification of goals is equivalent to assigning players to a sports team. Once the teams are decided, play can begin. In negotiation, "play" consists of trading off one goal compromise for another. The person who exacts the most advantageous compromises will have asked for more and gotten it.

Knowing what your and your opponent's goals are, knowing exactly what compromises have been agreed upon, and knowing what the individual and collective effects of those compromises are can make the difference between an effective and a misdirected negotiator.

To aid you in becoming more familiar with goals (your own and your opponent's) and to help you chart the course of goal compromises as the negotiation proceeds, I have devised a "goal-management diagram."

Before negotiation, before any goal compromises have been made, the individual horizontal goal-objective bars will be extended to the 100 per cent achievement position, representing your and your opponent's maximum expectation for each goal. In some cases your and your opponent's goals will be exact opposites (i.e., higher price vs. lower price), but often they will be totally independent goal objectives (i.e., convenient location, color preference, etc.). This is what the diagram looks like before the negotiation has begun:

GOAL–MANAGEMENT DIAGRAM BEFORE NEGOTIATION BEGINS

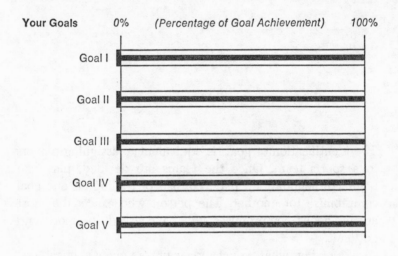

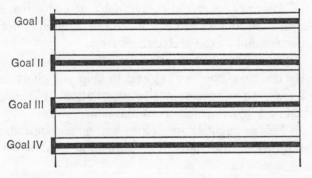

Our next diagram (p. 42) shows the goal compromises that might have been agreed on at the end of our model negotiation. As you can see, most goal-objective bars are no longer at the 100 per cent achievement line, and in fact one or two are at 0 per cent. In reading the diagram, it is important that you remember that a 45 per cent compromise in one goal is not equal to a 45 per cent compromise in another. Your No. I goal might be ten times as important as your No. V goal and therefore compromises in one cannot be balanced in a one-to-one ratio against the other. This diagram must be read *subjectively* and is only meant to help you see how compromises on a particular goal have left that goal objective relative to original expectations. In addition, goal-management diagrams prepared in the middle of a negotiation can be helpful in showing you what compromises to demand in negotiating future goal objectives and also the potential for advantageous modifications in prior goal compromises.

In preparing and using a goal-management diagram, it is important to remember that while it is prepared in terms of "your" and "your opponent's" goal objectives, deciding what your opponent's goals are is a subjective view based on whatever information you will have been able to gather prior to and during the negotiation. It will rarely actually represent what your opponent's goal objectives are (unless you are telepathic). If you knew exactly what they were, it would be equivalent to knowing what the down cards are in seven-card stud; the poker game would be over. Rather, the list of your opponent's goals is a "guesstimate" based on whatever information and hints you will have been able to determine to that point in the negotiation. It is entirely conceivable—in fact, probable—that as the negotiation proceeds you will identify and add goal objectives to your opponent's list. In the above negotiation, you will note we began with four opponent goals and ended with six.

GOAL–MANAGEMENT DIAGRAM AT END OF NEGOTIATION

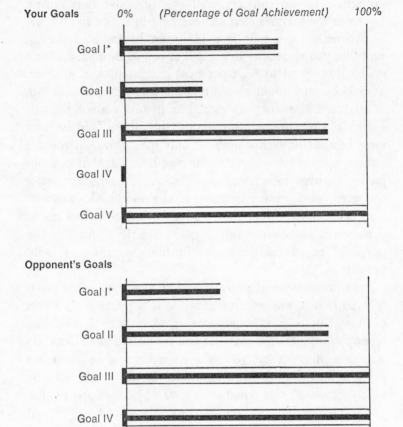

* These goals are counterbalancing goal objectives (an increase in your goal achievement will always cause a decrease in your opponent's goal achievement and vice versa).

Let us now see how the goal-management diagram is used to illustrate an actual negotiation. In the small community in which my coauthor Thomas Kiernan lives, there is a modest-sized store that sells groceries, meats and a general line of household staples. In a larger town five miles away there are two supermarkets which sell all these items at prices averaging between 15 and 20 per cent less than those of the smaller local store. For a long time Thomas made the ten-mile round trip three times a week to one of the larger supermarkets to do most of his shopping.

Finally, he went to see the owner of his local store and made him a proposition. Thomas explained to him that if he did his shopping regularly at the local store, it would cost him an average of $300 per month, whereas by going to the more distant supermarkets his monthly bill averaged only $240, saving him about $60, or 20 per cent, per month.

The store owner agreed with Thomas' figures, apologized for not being able to compete with the supermarkets, and indicated that considering what Thomas spent every month, he would like to have him as a steady customer. Thomas thereupon offered to transfer all his shopping from the supermarkets to the local store and to guarantee the owner $320 per month in purchases at his retail prices (this was the maximum monthly amount Thomas felt sure of spending), providing that the store owner would agree (1) to put Thomas on a monthly charge-account basis, and (2), after totaling up the bill at the end of each month, to deduct from it the 20 per cent Thomas would have saved by continuing to shop at the supermarkets.

Let's stop the action in this negotiation (which, incidentally, is one that actually occurred) and prepare a goal-management diagram (p. 44) from Thomas' point of view of the opening goals.

Thomas did not, of course, expect his request for a 20 per cent discount to go unchallenged, despite the basic ap-

GOAL-MANAGEMENT DIAGRAM • KIERNAN VS. LOCAL STORE

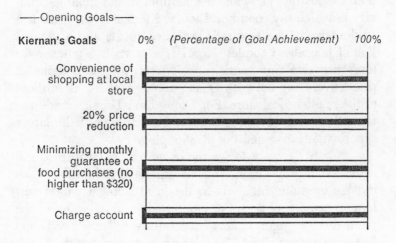

——Opening Goals——

Kiernan's Goals   0%   *(Percentage of Goal Achievement)*   *100%*

Convenience of shopping at local store

20% price reduction

Minimizing monthly guarantee of food purchases (no higher than $320)

Charge account

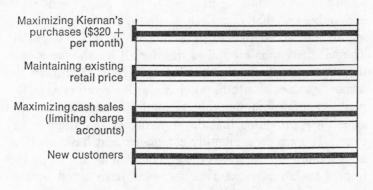

Local Store's Goals

Maximizing Kiernan's purchases ($320 + per month)

Maintaining existing retail price

Maximizing cash sales (limiting charge accounts)

New customers

peal of his offer. He knew, however, that the store owner was genuinely eager to have him as a free-spending customer and that the store owner was a businessman whose primary goals were new customers and increased sales. Thomas also knew that the store owner was astute enough to figure out that his 20 per cent savings at the supermarkets were somewhat compromised by the time, trouble, and mileage costs it took him to achieve them.

The store owner and Thomas proceeded to negotiate an agreement. The store owner consented to all of Thomas' other conditions provided that Thomas accept a 10 per cent monthly discount. Perhaps his counterproposal was designed to encourage Thomas to settle at a split-the-difference figure—a ploy of many amateur negotiators.

By splitting the difference, Thomas would have agreed to 15 per cent, but his calculations had shown him that the time, trouble, and mileage costs involved in shopping regularly at the supermarket had been eroding his 20 per cent savings by only 3 per cent over the course of a year. Hence Thomas decided to hold out for 17 per cent.

He explained this to his store owner friend (for by now they had become friends of sorts, the owner enjoying the negotiation as much as Thomas). Thomas said that ordinarily he would have gone no lower than 17 per cent. However, he added, because he believed a certain intangible pleasure would accrue to him from shopping regularly at the quaint local store, such pleasure was worth an additional percentage point to him. Therefore, he would be willing to close the agreement at 16 per cent.

The owner prolonged matters slightly by rejoining with an offer of 14 per cent, obviously still hoping that Thomas would come down to his original split-the-original-difference of 15 per cent.

By now Thomas was adamant about 16 per cent. So he came back with a revised proposal. He said that he would agree to 15 per cent, but only on $200 worth of guaranteed purchases a month. On all amounts over that, he wanted a 17 per cent discount. (With his expanding family and household needs, Thomas expected to spend close to $400 a month within a short time.)

The store owner quickly saw the folly of consenting to this arrangement and finally agreed to a blanket 16 per cent discount with $320 in guaranteed purchases. The following is a goal-management diagram of the final arrangement:

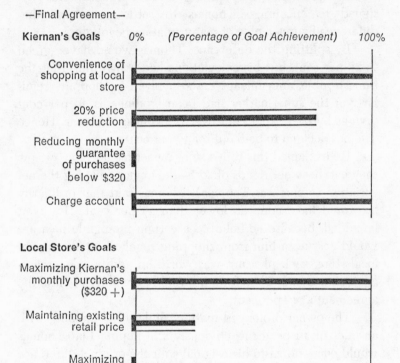

GOAL-MANAGEMENT DIAGRAM • KIERNAN VS. LOCAL STORE

—Final Agreement—

Kiernan's Goals   0%   *(Percentage of Goal Achievement)*   100%

- Convenience of shopping at local store
- 20% price reduction
- Reducing monthly guarantee of purchases below $320
- Charge account

Local Store's Goals

- Maximizing Kiernan's monthly purchases ($320 +)
- Maintaining existing retail price
- Maximizing cash sales
- New customers

As you can see from the diagram, goal compromises were made on both sides. Thomas got the convenience of doing all his shopping at the local store on a charge-account basis (a 100 per cent goal achievement for these two goals). In his goal of a 20 per cent price reduction, he succeeded to the tune of 80 per cent and got a 16 per cent price reduction. The one area in which he had to sacrifice his goal entirely was that of minimizing his guarantee of monthly purchases. Here he had to guarantee his full $320 per month worth of purchases.

The store keeper also won some and lost some. First and foremost, he got Thomas' business, guaranteed to the tune of $320 per month—100 per cent goal achievement on these two goals. He had to agree to allow Thomas to charge all his purchases (o per cent achievement on this goal) and had to agree to reduce prices 16 per cent (20 per cent achievement on his goal to not reduce prices at all relative to Thomas' request for a 20 per cent reduction).

I hope this anecdote, which is of a relatively simple negotiation, serves to make goal identification and management real to you. Although it involved a minimum of goal-objective modifications, it did include at least one, when Thomas reduced his request for a discount from 16 per cent to 15 per cent on only $200 worth of guaranteed purchases, but then asked for an increase to 17 per cent thereafter. Finally, it is an actual case history, which I hope will also serve to show you that the art of negotiation is one just as important to the average consumer as it is to people in business and professional life. I believe that the concepts presented in this book are universal and are equally applicable to the most sophisticated international armament negotiation as they are to purchasing agreements with your local store.

Part Four
STRATEGY

Chapter 6

Strategy: Common Ground and Linkage

Negotiation is in many senses a game. As such, it is best and most effectively played when a combination of strategy, tactics, and techniques are brought together to form a premeditated plan of action.

Those of you who play tennis or any other one-on-one sport in a serious way will be acutely aware of the usefulness of a "game plan." When you go out to compete against a particular opponent, you routinely assess his strengths and weaknesses and devise an over-all strategy with regard to how you are going to play against him. Against an opponent who is expert in all the strokes but is slow afoot or out of condition, your strategy might be to keep him running from one side of the court to the other. Against an opponent who is quick and nimble but who has a problematic backhand, you might plan to hit his backhand as often as you can. Against an opponent who depends on a powerful serve and a follow-up rush to the net, you might decide to concentrate on lob-returning his serve to keep him away from the net.

Negotiation also requires a game plan, one that brings together the elements of strategy, tactics, and techniques in the pursuit of "how to ask for more and get it." In the next few chapters I will be covering each element and trying to show how it can be effectively integrated into a "negotiating game plan."

Common Ground

In the beginning of any negotiation there will almost always be several goal objectives which are acceptable to both sides. The first element of any negotiating strategy should be to identify and isolate these goals as soon as possible so that they may be (1) used to establish the first base of "common ground," and (2) used later in conjunction with other tactics to negotiate the outcome of particular goal objectives. The point is to create a momentum of good will on which to begin to extract goal compromises and maximize your power to negotiate the critical compromises of the exchange.

By way of example, let's assume you have just applied for a mortgage at your bank. You know that the bank's going interest rate for home mortgages is 8½ per cent. You also know that this same rate is applied by all other banks in your community. This rate is acceptable to you; your concern is whether you can obtain a thirty-year mortgage when the bank has indicated that it deals only in twenty-year mortgages. Your negotiation with the bank will thus begin with the 8½ per cent interest rate being common ground between you. You may subsequently wish to ignore any further discussion of the 8½ per cent figure. Or you may choose to use it in some way to persuade the bank to be more flexible in its twenty-year policy. For instance, you may volunteer to pay an 8¾ per cent interest rate if the bank grants you a thirty-year pay-back time. Or you may seek to negotiate an interest rate lower than the conventional 8½ per cent if the bank remains inflexible in its twenty-year rule.

Common ground is extremely important, because your opponents' willingness to concede goal objectives is usually directly proportionate to the common ground that has been established between you. Hence the first stage in any negotiating strategy should be to establish as much common ground between you and your opponent as possible.

Generally, until the maximum amount of common ground has been established, it is a good idea to refrain from pressing any primary goal objectives that you feel will be difficult for your opponent to accept.

Each time agreement is reached on a goal, further common ground has been added to the negotiation. Indeed, the end result of a completed negotiation is the reaching of common ground on all objectives. It is therefore wise, when planning a negotiating strategy, to expect to work gradually from "outside in." That is, you should establish as much of the common ground between you and your opponent as possible at the beginning and then try to keep forming more and more common ground as you approach the most difficult or contentious issues between you.

In the course of a negotiation, it is not unusual for a particular goal objective to come up for discussion for which no goal compromise seems possible. Each side has presented its opening position, its rationales, and counterrationales and compromises have been suggested. But no compromise is found which seems acceptable to both sides over the particular goal objective, and the negotiation becomes deadlocked.

Whenever this occurs, the discussion of the particular goal objective should be adjourned until all other goal objectives have been agreed on. Invariably, in my experience, at the end of the negotiation, with a mass of common ground having been accumulated between the parties, a great deal more compromise will be possible on the seemingly unresolvable goal. In nine out of ten cases, an acceptable goal compromise will be found.

Alternatively, the resolution of a stubborn goal compromise may be held in abeyance until another disputed goal issue comes up, about which you are willing to make some concessions. When you reach one of these goals, you can then "link" your concessions on this goal to your opponent's willingness to make concessions on the prior disputed goal. In this way you can often give away something of minor importance to gain something of major importance.

Linkage

Linkage in negotiation was recently brought into the headlines by President Jimmy Carter. In the area of United States foreign policy, he has linked the resolution of many issues to the so-called "human rights" objective. In return for compromise on certain foreign policy interests, President Carter is insisting that the countries involved maintain minimum human rights standards. He is using international economic or strategic goals to win compromise on other goals which he feels are important and on which he was finding it difficult to achieve independent compromise. However, one doesn't have to be President to employ goal linkage.

Let's look at common ground and linkage at work in our negotiation for a thirty-year 8½ per cent mortgage. You have agreed to buy the house in question for $100,000. The bank usually limits mortgages to either 75 per cent of the purchase price or 75 per cent of the market value that the bank's appraisers assign to the house, whichever is less at 8½ per cent, payable in twenty years.

Seventy-five per cent of $100,000 is $75,000. But you need $85,000 in mortgage money and explain your needs to the bank officer to whom you have gone to open your mortgage discussion.

The officer, knowing the policy of the bank, cautions that you are not likely to get the bank to agree to an $85,000 mortgage. Nevertheless, he urges you to submit your application anyway, on the chance that the bank's appraisers will value the house at a figure higher than the $100,000 purchase price.

The appraisers subsequently place a $115,000 value on the house. The officer calls to tell you that your request for $85,000 has been approved, but that they will not go beyond a twenty-five-year term.

Why did they agree to the higher amount? Your application produced very favorable information about your financial responsibility and credit record. Coupled with that was their $115,000 appraisal figure. The common ground created by the achievement of two of the bank's goal objectives (credit rating and appraisal) caused them to compromise on the amount of the loan. In turn, you were willing to compromise the term goal when it was linked with the higher face amount you were seeking.

Let's look at this negotiation in terms of goal-management diagrams (pp. 56–57) and analyze how and why the respective goal compromises were made.

What occurred here was that the bank, on the basis of its achievement of certain important informational goals (your good credit rating, the appraised value of the house), was able to establish a good deal more common ground between itself and you than existed at the beginning of your discussion. Using this common ground, it linked its informational goals to your and its primary goals and decided that in view of your willingness to concede to its goal of the

GOAL–MANAGEMENT DIAGRAM

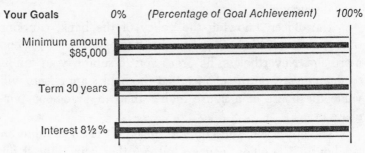

-Prior to Negotiation-

Your Goals   0%   *(Percentage of Goal Achievement)*   100%

Minimum amount $85,000

Term 30 years

Interest 8½%

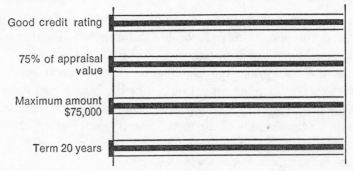

Bank's Goals

Good credit rating

75% of appraisal value

Maximum amount $75,000

Term 20 years

twenty-five-year mortgage term, it could concede to your primary goal of $85,000.

The end result was that while you compromised on a secondary goal (thirty years), the bank yielded on a primary goal ($75,000). Upon the conclusion of the negotiation you had asked for more and gotten it. Only, however, because the bank was practiced in the functions of common ground and goal linkage.

GOAL-MANAGEMENT DIAGRAM

After the Negotiation-

Your Goals   0%   *(Percentage of Goal Achievement)*   *100%*

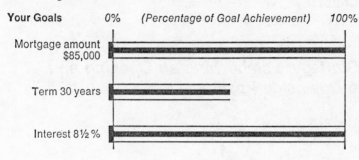

| Mortgage amount $85,000 |
| Term 30 years |
| Interest 8½% |

Bank's Goals

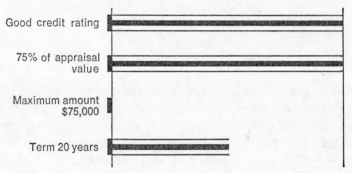

| Good credit rating |
| 75% of appraisal value |
| Maximum amount $75,000 |
| Term 20 years |

These two processes, then, should be the basis of all your negotiating strategy. You should at first set out to establish as much common ground as possible between you and your opponent, and you should continually expand on it as the negotiation progresses.

Chapter 7

Strategy: Establishing an Opening and a Downside Position

For the purpose of formulating our strategy for reaching our opening (maximum) and downside (minimum) positions, we can now distill the broad mix of goals described previously into two groups: essential, or primary, goals; and nonessential, or secondary, goals. Essential, or primary, goals will be those which you consider vital to your interests in the exchange and which you will be least likely to be flexible about. Nonessential, or secondary, goals will be those that are less vital to your interests, and on which you are more willing to compromise or concede altogether.

Scaling Your Goals

In relating goals to strategy and in order to establish opening and downside positions, it will be necessary to further define your goals in terms of *a quantitative scale that represents your maximum and minimum expectations* for each goal.

Let's suppose you are looking for a new job. Your primary/essential goals are these:

1. *Salary:* $20,000 per year.

2. *Career change:* You have been working as an outside salesman for a large computer company. You are bored with computers, have always wanted to work in advertising—eventually as a copywriter—and have decided to concentrate your job search on advertising agencies.

Your secondary/nonessential goals are:

3. *Proximity to where you live:* You would like to keep your commuting to less than fifteen minutes each way.

4. *Job opportunity:* You would like to work for a small firm run by relatively young staff and with strong growth potential.

5. *Vacation:* Your present job provides you with a three-week annual vacation, and you would prefer in your new job to get at least the same.

You have found three advertising agencies interested in discussing a job with you. When you go in for your interviews, you should be prepared to negotiate. Part of that strategy should consist of your having in mind the quantitative range that represents, for each goal, your maximum expectation, which you tell your opponent, and your minimum expectation, which you keep to yourself.

What is the maximum salary you feel you could command at the moment? What is the minimum you would accept if all other factors about the new job seem right?

Would you consider other than a copywriting job?

What is the longest commuting time you could conceive of for the right job?

Would you consider a large advertising agency or is a small one a firmly fixed criterion?

What is the minimum vacation arrangement you would accept? Would you take two weeks if the other factors were favorable?

Looking back at your list of goals, I have quantified each goal in accordance with the maximum-minimum rule. First, your primary goals:

1. *Salary: $17,500 to $23,000 (goal: $20,000).* You are presently earning $18,500. In transferring to a new job, you would love an income increase. You have also learned that the going rate for copywriters averages out to $23,000. Taking into account the fact that you are a newcomer to advertising, you are not realistically expecting to be offered the going rate right off the bat. If the right job opportunity presented itself, you might even accept a beginning salary as low as $17,500 just to get your foot in the door.

2. *Position: Any in advertising (goal: copywriter).* You would like to begin directly as a copywriter, but you know that most agencies do not hire beginners in this craft. Thus you are prepared to consider any job in advertising just to get into the industry.

Secondary goals:

3. *Commuting time: Up to forty-five minutes each way (goal: fifteen minutes).*

4. *Job opportunity: In any advertising agency (goal: in a small firm).* You prefer a small, growing agency because you feel that such a working milieu will provide you with the best opportunity to get ahead. However, you realize that small agencies are less likely to hire advertising beginners than are large ones. So you have not dismissed the possibility of ending up in a large agency.

5. *Vacation: Two to four weeks (goal: three weeks).*

By defining your goals as to their respective ranges, you are now in a position to negotiate your job prospects. Suppose you do get a nibble from a small agency. Their terms: start as a copywriting assistant at $18,000 a year, with four weeks' vacation and an office less than fifteen minutes away.

Then you get another offer, this one from a large agency an hour away. Their terms: start as a space salesman at $20,000 a year plus commissions, with four weeks' vacation.

Finally, you get a third offer from a medium-sized agency thirty minutes away. Their terms: copywriter on their computer-company account at $15,000 a year, with two weeks' vacation.

Each has its attractions within the framework of your goal ranges. The first meets your small-agency criterion (secondary goal) and at least partially fulfills your two primary goals. The vacation conditions (secondary goal) are more than you hoped for and the commuting requirements (secondary goal) is satisfied.

The second meets your salary requirements (primary goal) and exceeds your vacation hopes (secondary goal), but falls short in other important respects.

The third comes up short on salary (primary goal) and

vacation (secondary goal) but is perhaps the best in terms of job opportunity.

Three job offers. And that is what they are: offers. In other words, invitations to negotiate.

You would be foolish to accept any of these offers as presented. In each case you could probably negotiate substantially better terms for yourself. By clearly knowing what you want—by having a maximum-minimum range in your goal structure—you could improve on each situation.

Take the first offer, for instance. The salary is short of your salary goal and you would start only as an assistant copywriter. If I were negotiating for you, I would try to get you another $2,000 per year by giving up a week's vacation. In that way you would come close to your salary goal objective while still fulfilling your vacation time goal. Moreover, I would insist that you be moved up to a full-fledged copywriter's position within six months, provided that your work was satisfactory, with a commensurate increase in salary.

In the second instance, the problem is not salary but job type. You have no interest in being a salesman in a large agency, even though the $20,000-plus-commission arrangement provides you with the potential to make much more money than you expected. I would come back with a counteroffer to accept the $20,000 but forego the commission and perhaps two weeks of vacation time, in exchange for being placed in a copywriting job. If the agency agreed, you would have fulfilled your two primary goals while conceding on your secondary objectives.

In the case of the third offer, everything is fairly well balanced vis-à-vis your goal ranges except for salary and vacation time. If I were you, this is the job I would go after, since they have offered you a full-time copywriting position in a field with which you are familiar. The salary, however, is below your downside position. I would make use of your expertise in computers, plus the fact of the reduced vacation time, to negotiate a higher starting salary—say, $18,000. (I would not start out by asking for $18,000; instead, I would ask for $20,000, pointing out that even this is below the going rate.) Most likely, the agency will agree to $18,000. Thus your two primary goals would be largely met (salary is above your downside position), while your secondary goals would be only partially yielded.

Opening Position

The purpose of quantifying your goals into scales of maximum and minimum expectation is to provide you with a third important component of strategy. This consists of your two basic negotiating positions: (1) your opening position; (2) your downside position.

Simply stated, your opening position should encompass the maximum that you want to achieve from an exchange. Many people are nervous or apprehensive about establishing an opening position that reflects their highest hopes. They fear that they will be laughed at or that such boldness will queer the deal before it begins.

This is nonsense. So long as your highest hopes are realistic—and it is the process of quantifying your goals into maximum-minimum ranges that will keep them so—there is little to fear in presenting your opening position in the strongest terms possible.

Most likely, your opening position will not be agreed to. However, you can be confident that it will elicit a response which will give you some idea of your opponent's range.

Downside Position

A downside position, unlike an opening position, should never be revealed to your opponent. In a sense, it is the level which each side in a negotiation is trying to discover in the other. It is the lowest point of compromise each side has set for itself for each of its goals. In some cases it will be close to one's opening position, in others it may be a willingness to sacrifice the particular goal in its entirety.

Of course, the fact that one has set a particular level as a minimum point of compromise does not mean that one will be willing to accept that level of compromise for each of one's goal objectives or that one's downside position is inviolate. Rather, it represents a "danger" level below which under normal circumstances one should not compromise. In a negotiation, it should act as an alarm to alert us that we are reaching below the minimum level that prenegotiation logic determined.

To sum this chapter up, the second element in preparing a negotiating strategy consists of three interrelated items:

1. Formulate a maximum-minimum scale for each of your goals.

2. Arrange your goal maximums into an opening position which you can then manipulate through concession and compromise, as the negotiation progresses, to get what you realistically want.

3. Arrange your goal minimums into a downside position, below which you will not under most circumstances go and against which you can measure the effectiveness of your side of the negotiation.

Chapter 8

Strategy: Style and Power

A recent issue of *Motor Trend* magazine reported on a study, conducted by a midwestern university, having to do with the relationship between the appearance of consumers and the quality of treatment they receive on the part of those who sell to them.

One aspect of the study led to some interesting conclusions about the effects of mode of dress and general appearance on new-car prices, as well as the effects of sex and race. In this part of the study, seven people posing as new-car buyers each visited some twenty Ford, Plymouth, and Chevrolet dealers in a certain area in the Midwest. Each asked a salesman for a price on a full-size, two-door hardtop of the respective makes, with the same equipment. The "buyers" were all about the same age and included (1) a poorly dressed and somewhat scruffy-looking white male; (2) a well-dressed, neatly groomed white male; (3) a poorly dressed black male; (4) a well-dressed black male;

(5) a poorly dressed white female; (6) a well-dressed white female; and (7) a sloppily dressed Oriental male.

In every case, each of the "buyers" was offered the same cars at different prices. The findings of the study showed that the well-dressed and neatly groomed white and black males were consistently quoted the lowest price figures. The sex of the "buyer" had little or no impact on the prices, although in the case of the women, the well-dressed one was consistently given a lower price. The poorly dressed black was offered higher prices than the poorly dressed white (but not much higher), and both were consistently given considerable steeper quotations than the well-dressed individuals. The prices to the badly dressed Oriental were the highest of all. Presumably, the study concluded, a shave, haircut, and good suit might result in a lower car price.

The findings of this university study are not unusual. Numerous academic and business surveys conducted over the last decade or so have revealed without question that a definite cause-and-effect relationship based on dress and appearance exists between sellers and buyers and the financial outcome of their exchanges. In short, the more solid and respectable you appear, the better you will make out in the market place.

On the basis of my own experience I can, to a certain extent, endorse these findings as they apply to negotiation. However, it is not solely a particular mode of dress, length of hair, or general appearance that will reinforce your negotiating power. Rather, it is your total persona that will add to or detract from your effectiveness. Your personal style—of communicating and otherwise handling yourself—is an integral part of the impression you make on your opponent. Dress often helps to convey our personal style, but just as often it can be misleading. Howard Hughes negotiated for many years in sneakers and tattered shirts, yet he never had much difficulty getting what he wanted. Why? Because his eccentric dress tended to emphasize, rather than distract from, his real power.

In his best-selling book *Power*, Michael Korda discourses on the mechanics of becoming important and powerful in the business world. An essential part of the reality of power, he says (with, I would hope, tongue in cheek), is the illusion one is able to create of one's power. To be powerful, in other words, one must give the *appearance* of power.

Korda counsels that if you want to make it up the corporate ladder into the executive suite or if you wish to become an independent tycoon, you should outfit yourself early on in your career with the trappings of success and importance. This means holding negotiating meetings in your office where your co-operative secretary can intermittently interrupt you with urgent "phone calls" from London or Paris. It means decking yourself out in a Cartier tank watch and Gucci loafers. It means possessing a large desk whose highly rubbed surface is bare save for a gold Tiffany pen-and-pencil set and a color-co-ordinated, twenty-line telephone apparatus that looks like the inertial-guidance computer on a Boeing 747. It means having bribed the *maître d'* at an exclusive restaurant to address you by name when you bring customers to lunch and then having him bring you a telephone to answer an "urgent overseas" call placed by your still-willing secretary from a luncheonette a few blocks away.

The trappings of power, says Korda, do more than anything else to convince people you are powerful—that is, that you have the power to bring about important decisions and put deals into motion.

Alas, I have negotiated on countless occasions with such power-image creators. And I can tell you that their real power is almost always inversely proportional to their trappings. Power-image people are usually so preoccupied with maintaining or improving their images that they tend to give away more than they demand. In the superficial impression they seek to impart, their style is all. Rather than be tough on terms, they become preoccupied with flashing their power symbols.

A fashionable watch, Gucci loafers, and a space-age telephone console do not a negotiator make! They represent an attempt to intimidate negotiating opponents into being more pliable. Against an experienced negotiator, they are about as effective as using a rubber knife to slice bread.

By using style as an integral part of a negotiating strategy, then, I do not mean affected lifestyles or carefully carved impressions thereof.

What I mean by "style" is the general way you conduct yourself in a negotiation. Intimidation can occasionally be useful, but only at selected moments. Style can include intimidation, but it also includes persuasion, surprise, amiability, articulation, secretiveness, diversion, and so on.

Style, in essence, is the sum total of your personality and character traits as they apply in an adversary situation, which a negotiation is. If you are articulate but weak-willed, you may start out a negotiation well but end it badly. If you are inarticulate but persistent, you may start out badly but end well.

Basically, your style cannot be created. It is already part of you, and you will function in a negotiation just as you do in other areas of your life. Style nevertheless is extremely important in negotiation, and if you tend in real life to be excitable, to get easily hurt or discouraged, or to be personally vindictive, then you will not do well when you bring these traits to a negotiation.

Although your personal style—that is, your personality and disposition—can not be remolded to any significant degree, it can be modified or "edited" for negotiating purposes. If you have a shrill voice, you should try to moderate it. If

your everyday speech is habitually peppered with exple-
tives, you should put a rein on the habit when you are asking for more.

Nervous tics, an incessantly demanding tone of voice, a
tendency to talk in a superior or condescending manner—
these and many more facets of one's personal style can easily
get in the way of effective negotiation.

To a certain extent, you should endeavor to tailor your
style to your opponent, as well as to the issues at stake. People tend to feel most comfortable talking and dealing with
people like themselves.

I have a friend who, after a long struggle, has finally
become a successful manager of a rock music group. He
comes from a very cultivated family, is a graduate of a top
eastern law school, and for some time practiced law as an
associate and budding partner in one of New York's leading
blue-chip firms. Tiring of corporate legal work, he decided
to make his way in the rock music world as a manager and
legal adviser. He quit his job with the law firm and began to
circulate among musicians, agents, and promoters in search
of clients. Retaining his professional, lawyerly manner of
speech, he at first found it impossible to find musician-
clients. When he finally did sign up a client, he discovered
that other more "hip" music managers and promoters were
reluctant to do business with him.

One day I noticed an abrupt change in my friend's
manner of talking. Suddenly he was no longer speaking in
the civilized tones of academe. Instead, his speech was the
jive argot of the music world. When I asked him what ac-
counted for the radical change, he explained. When he went
to a rock promoter to negotiate a deal for his client in his
lawyerly style of speech, the promoters refused to negotiate
with him. He was young like them, but in every other way
he appeared different. It was only when he started to speak

their language that he began to find easy connections and was able to negotiate profitable deals. Thereafter, several well-known musicians sought him out to manage them.

I am not suggesting that you change yourself so radically. In negotiating, you should always be yourself. But you should also be sensitive to your opponent and his or her personality and disposition. And you should make this sensitivity a vital component of your strategy in any negotiation.

Chapter 9

Strategy: Whom to Negotiate With

I would not be telling you anything new if I said modern
life is complex and often tends to obscure the obvious. Very
often determining whom we are negotiating with is not the
straightforward question it might appear.

How frequently I've found myself in a negotiation with
someone and, after making an offer I felt should have
clinched the deal, heard my opponent say, "Sounds good to
me, but let me check it out with my partner." What partner?
Up until then I thought my opponent was a sole principal.

Or how about the company vice-president who has
been extracting compromise after compromise from you,
then, when it comes time to sign the final purchase order,
says, "If it was up to me, I'd jump at it, but I've got to clear
it with my group manager." What group manager? Up until
this point he has been negotiating as hard and fast as if he
had the authority to place the order himself.

Probably an overwhelming majority of negotiations in

modern life occur through an intermediary who is not a full or even partial principal to the negotiation. In their most formal appearances, these intermediaries (or "shields," as I shall call them) are brokers, lawyers, and agents of various kinds. However, shields can just as easily be bureaucrats, salesmen, or company executives—in fact, anyone who is party to a negotiation but does not have the complete authority to decide all goal compromises to the negotiation is, for our purposes, a shield.

As frustrating as shields can be when we are negotiating against one, they often fulfill a very useful function, both in bringing the exchange into existence and in negotiating its conclusion. Furthermore, when the tables are turned and a shield is acting on your behalf, he or she can be a very effective part of *your* negotiating strategy.

Shields as "Exchange Makers"

Agent or broker shields often function as "exchange makers" by organizing and centralizing a diffuse market. A classic example is the real estate broker who is familiar with and lists all offerings of property in a given area. A potential buyer can go to the real estate broker, state his needs, and be offered in one stop what might take weeks if not months of searching alone. Similarly, the seller can use the broker as a central listing point from which to solicit buyers, rather than use the hit-or-miss approach of a "for sale" sign on the lawn or classified ad in the local newspaper.

The second function shields fulfill as exchange makers is to help their clients—buyers or sellers—establish realistic goals for the contemplated exchange. Realistic goal establishment is often an inexact endeavor for which no fixed references exist. Because shields are intimately familiar with their market, they are in a much better position, to help you establish realistic goal objectives, whereas your own guess-timate might be unrealistically high or low.

One of my key functions as a literary agent is helping my clients determine what a realistic royalty guarantee for a given book should be. Royalty advances (guarantees) range from $2,500 to $2,500,000. What makes one book worth thousands and the next, hundreds of thousands? Ask for less than the market warrants and you could leave yourself out of pocket a relative fortune; ask for too much and you could end up with an unpublished manuscript. Unrealistically high goals can pre-empt a negotiation, and unrealistically low ones can deprive you of your rightful share.

Shields can also be helpful in minimizing conflicts over secondary-goal compromises by pointing out "standard practices" to the parties in a given exchange. I recall my indignation when the seller's attorney in my first real estate purchase asked me to pay him $125 for preparing a purchase-money mortgage. I told him that he wasn't representing me and that he should get his fee from his own client—it wasn't the money, it was the principle! I quickly did a 180-degree turnabout when my attorney told me that, indeed, it was standard practice for the buyer to pay for the preparation of the purchase-money mortgage and that I should write the seller's attorney a check.

Finally, shields are often essential to a negotiation because of their legal or other expertise.

Five years ago Charles, a friend of mine, was divorced. Prior to the split he "negotiated" his own separation-divorce agreement with his wife. His wife, however, did her negotiating through a lawyer. Charles, hoping to save himself some money, chose to go it himself and planned to hire a lawyer only to handle the legal mechanics of the actual divorce.

Since securing the divorce, Charles has been forced to spend close to $20,000 in legal fees in his attempts to redress what he now knows is the totally unfavorable agreement he signed with his ex-wife. Had he spent $500 for a competent lawyer's "shield" services during the negotiating period, he would not be out of pocket $20,000 today.

One lawyer I know has a motto, "If they don't hire me now, they'll be back later and with twice the business." Unfortunate, but true.

The Strategy of "Shielding"

Now let's take a look at the shield tactic as it might be used against us. I remember an experience early in my negotiating career which illustrates shielding at its most lethal.

The negotiation involved a mortgage on one of the first buildings I ever owned. The mortgage was coming due and I requested the standard mortgage extension, which normally would have been granted more or less automatically. As I prepared to fill out the application for the extension, Sam, the bank's mortgage officer, called to say that the bank wanted a paydown on the mortgage's face amount of between 6 and 10 per cent. If I agreed, it would expedite the bank's approval of my extension request.

I agreed to an 8 per cent paydown and sent Sam my application reflecting the reduction. I heard nothing from the bank for a couple of weeks. Since time was running short, I called Sam to learn what was causing the delay. He told me that he had submitted my application to the bank's loan committee for "final approval" and that it had sent it back with a request for a 15 per cent paydown.

By then it was too late for me to find another bank to take over the mortgage. I had been the victim of the shield factor. I had been led to believe by the principal's shield (Sam) that an 8 per cent paydown would produce the extension I wanted. I was later told that I could only get the extension if I payed off double the amount I had originally agreed to. Having secured my compromise to one level of paydown, the loan committee was able to push me to a further concession by refusing to stand by the goal compromise set up by its shield.

There ought to be a law against "double negotiation," as there is for double jeopardy. But there isn't. A shield is often used to "test the waters" of an exchange. By giving tentative agreement to goal concessions, shields establish common ground from which to proceed, while leaving final agreement and/or ratification subject to the approval of their principal. After all issues have been apparently settled, the committee returns to indicate that one or two goal agreements are still not satisfactory to its principal. Relying on the common ground established, a further degree of compromise is usually extracted.

The only defense against a double-negotiating opponent is to refuse to renegotiate prior goal agreements without extracting counterbalancing concessions—in effect, to say that if your opponent wishes to renegotiate a particular goal compromise, then you in turn have several other goal compromises which you are no longer comfortable with and wish to rediscuss.

Double negotiation is, however, only one of the many tactics that shields commonly use. The following are several others.

Shields and principals sometimes work together in a conspiratorial manner, copying the classic "good guy-bad guy" techniques of police interrogation. This form of interrogation involves two policemen—usually detectives—who take turns questioning a suspect. One is harsh, loud, and threatening. The other is gentle, sympathetic, and comforting. The threatening interrogator will lead off, terrorizing the suspect with intimations of physical violence and incessant shouting. The other detective will appear to have to restrain his partner, possibly even "ordering" him out of the room until he "pulls himself together." The gentle detective will then, through his calm and sympathetic questioning, attempt to win the suspect over to his side. Before the first interrogator can return with more threats and physical intimidation, the suspect is liable to confess to the sympathetic one.

Police interrogation is a form of negotiation. When principals and shields work together in a negotiation, they often employ similar techniques. The shield may appear as the hard bargainer, trying to strip you of all your goals and expectations, only to have his position softened at the last moment by the principal, who throws in a few conciliatory concessions to keep you interested, or vice versa.

Another common shield tactic is for him or her to feign ignorance of, or actually be ignorant of, certain information that you require to negotiate effectively—information a principal might legally or ethically be required to reveal if he or she negotiated directly with you.

This is a common ploy of real estate brokers. Suppose, say, you have found a house you really want to buy. Usually, you will have to negotiate through a broker representing the seller. You have inspected the house and are generally satisfied with it, but have noticed traces of stains on the ceilings of the upstairs bedrooms. You ask the broker if the house has a leaky roof. If it does, you plan to scale down your offer by a couple of thousand dollars and use the difference to have the roof repaired.

The broker promises to find out. The next day you're told that the seller says the stains are not from a leaky roof, but are discolorations resulting from the cheap ceiling paint used by a previous owner.

You therefore make the higher offer and a deal is eventually concluded. You move into your new house. Two weeks later there is a heavy rainstorm. Suddenly the ceilings in the upstairs rooms come crashing down in a soggy mess of plaster. Through the gaping holes in the ceiling you can see water cascading through the underside of the roof. You have the roof repaired and are presented with a $5,000 repair bill.

Of course, had you first spoken directly to the seller about the condition, there is no guarantee that he might not have lied to you outright about it. However, it is not as likely as the broker who, when subsequently confronted with the facts, can simply shrug his shoulders and claim to have no control over the information that was given to him. The intermediary effect is to set up a convenient excuse for "misunderstandings"—it's equivalent to the guy who pays his bills late and then blames it on the mails.

Shield Hierachies

In addition to individual shields, when dealing with bureaucracies or large corporations you will often find yourself negotiating through a group of shields—a hierarchy of individuals each of whom has relatively more authority than the person below him. You may begin the negotiation with a junior executive who will have to refer the more substantive goal compromises to his superiors. As your requests become more stringent, the superior will refer the concession decisions to a senior executive who might then bring them to the still higher level of the executive committee, and so on.

Since any goal agreements are essentially decisions, it is necessary in planning your strategy to consider the question of who, at what level, will have to approve the goal agreements involved in your negotiation. Usually, the person you begin the negotiation with will have the authority to reach agreements only within limited goal ranges. Or he will have the authority to *recommend* a goal-agreement package to the higher-echelon decision makers which will routinely be accepted. If you plan on asking for more in the way of goal agreements than your beginning shield-opponent has the power to grant unilaterally, then you can expect the negotiation either to be terminated or referred to a higher authority.

In planning your strategy, then, you should take into account the advisability of using the beginning shield-opponent to establish as much common ground as possible so that when the more crucial aspects of the negotiation are kicked upstairs, the higher authority will be encouraged to strive for an agreement.

EXAMPLE:

You apply for a personal loan at the bank. Provided that your credit information falls within certain guidelines, the bank officer recommends your loan to the loan committee, which will normally approve any loan the officer recommends so long as it is in accordance with the bank's regular policies vis-à-vis such loans—that is, amounts, interest rates, repayment schedules, and so on.

But suppose you request an interest rate or face amount that exceeds the bank's regular policies? In such a case, you can expect the bank officer to say that he will have to make a special presentation to the loan committee. Because you have already established a lot of common ground in your initial negotiations with the officer, chances are that he will be willing to make an extra effort to persuade the committee to make an exception to its normal loan policies.

The position of an opponent negotiating on behalf of a hierarchy is the same as that of any shield, with one exception. Often hierarchies are structured so that the person you are negotiating with will receive recognitional responsibility for the agreement (good or bad) that he brings about. In other words, if the deal is a good one, the lower-echelon per-

son will be recognized as having been responsible for bringing it about. If the deal turns sour, he or she will be blamed.

However, the person's superiors or the decision-making
level to which he or she has to go for approval, will not be
credited directly for the good deal. But they will be held responsible for the deal if it turns sour.

EXAMPLE:

The personal loan officer at your bank is judged on
the total number of successful loans he initiates. The
officer's loan record does not, however, reflect directly
on the members of the loan committee, which gives
final approval for the officer's loans. Nevertheless, if a
loan goes bad, you can be sure that someone superior to
the committee in the bank's hierarchy will want to
know why the committee approved it.

Thus the hierarchy has less interest in approving a goal
compromise that may be speculative, since it will be held to
account if it turns out badly, but will only be given marginal
recognition if it succeeds.

In addition, when structuring goal objectives that will
have to be referred to a hierarchy, it is important to keep
in mind that the common ground achieved in a negotiation
with a shield will carry less weight than common ground in
which the decision makers have a direct interest. Because of
this, it may be wise to keep as many of your goal objectives
within the goal range of your opponent, since further concessions may be difficult to get. The higher level, which has
shielded itself from you, has as its primary purpose protecting itself from approving speculative goal compromises. The
more your opponent has to refer goal concessions to the
higher level, the more the higher level is likely to resist
them.

EXAMPLE:

You are a good customer and the loan officer at the bank likes you. The loan committee of this branch can approve loans up to $10,000. You have asked for a loan of $12,000. Such a request must be referred to the main branch. The committee that reviews it there will have little interest in your relationship with the branch officer. It will have no common-ground relationship with you. It is therefore likely to turn down your application for $12,000.

Goal concessions that have to be referred to a higher authority should be restricted to the most substantive ones. The hierarchy tends to see only the goal disagreements in an ongoing negotiation, not the goal agreements. Too many referrals will make them despair of the possibility of ever reaching a reasonable agreement or any agreement whatsoever.

EXAMPLE:

The bank officer tells you that the bank's normal rate of interest is 9 per cent and the maximum length of repayment is one year. You want an 8½ per cent rate and a two-year pay-back period. Both concession requests will have to be referred to the main branch loan committee. They may approve the two-year concession, but it is extremely unlikely that it will grant an 8½ per cent interest rate. Or vice versa. By dropping one request, the question of the other will seem more legitimate and the committee may well approve it.

In some negotiations you may have the choice of dealing directly with either a higher level of the hierarchy or a lower level. In some cases it will be to your advantage to choose the higher level, which possesses greater authority to make a wider range of goal concessions without referring them to still higher levels. In others, it may be better to deal with the lower level. Although its goal ranges and goal-concession authority might be more limited, it is likely to comprise less skilled negotiators.

A danger in choosing to pursue a negotiation at too high a hierarchal level is that you will be referred back to a lower level if it is decided that the matter does not warrant the time of the senior person to whom you have gone. Although a subordinate may be diligent in engaging in the negotiation because it has been referred by a superior, he may resent the fact that you did not come to him in the first place and therefore be more rigid in his goal concessions.

EXAMPLE:

You have both business and personal loan accounts with the bank. Your business accounts are handled by Mr. Blackman, a senior vice-president at the bank's main office. Your personal accounts are handled by Mr. Horskins, a junior loan officer at your local branch. You need an urgent personal loan with some special conditions and you want quicker action than you normally get when you go through Horskins. So you apply for the loan through Blackman.

Blackman, since he does not involve himself in personal loans, will refer the loan down to Horskins. Horskins, insulted that you went over his head on a matter that was his provenance, will be inclined to stall your loan and the granting of the special requests.

Learning to "place your shots" when dealing with a shield hierarchy can mean the difference between success and failure. Pursuing your goal objectives on the right level with the right person can be a prerequisite to successfully asking for more and getting it.

Chapter 10

Strategy: Where and When

Where

The location of a negotiation may be of little strategic significance in one instance. In another, it may be of great importance.

In international relations, the decision about where to negotiate is often a ticklish and involved one. It usually requires extensive negotiations of its own. The difficulties, concessions, and agreements reached on "where" are sometimes portents of the outcome of the actual exchange. You may recall that the diplomatic convolutions preceding the Vietnam Peace Conference over the question of where the conference should take place required months of negotiation between the parties and a number of mediators.

The location in which you negotiate can be significant in several ways. One is that the location might reveal the financial or other circumstances of one of the parties—circumstances that can be used to shape you or your opponent's strategy and tactics.

In many negotiations, I often travel to my opponent's premises—whether an office, home, or other site that holds clues to his or her circumstances. By so doing, I can make many useful and accurate decisions about the opponent's goal ranges. I can also determine to what extent my opponent is an image maker betraying a basic insecurity.

I recall a negotiation with a film producer who had come to New York from Los Angeles to negotiate a motion picture contract for one of my client's books. The producer took a large penthouse suite at one of New York's poshest hotels and invited me up for an initial, get-acquainted breakfast meeting. Having only spoken to him on the phone, I was happy to accept his invitation.

When I arrived at the suite I was let in by an attractive "secretary." The producer greeted me effusively. Our meeting was interrupted by the usual spate of urgent calls "from the coast." I didn't like the guy from the start and wasn't impressed by his pomp.

Three more negotiating sessions ensued at the suite. Tentative agreement was reached, and the producer promised to mail me a contract the next day from Hollywood, to which he said he was returning that night.

The next day the manager of the hotel called me at my office. A piece of paper with my name on it had been found in the producer's suite. He wondered if I could tell him of the whereabouts of Mr. Producer. It seemed that he and his "secretary" had left the hotel without formally checking out or paying their bill. Needless to say, I never received the contract he had promised.

Another significance of location lies in its convenience and comfort factor. I know a man who absolutely refuses to negotiate anywhere except at the bar of his country club after a pleasant round of golf with his negotiating opponent. When I asked him why, he said it is because that is where he is most comfortable doing business. He uses the golf game to begin the negotiation and then exploits the clubby atmosphere of the nineteenth hole to press home his essential goals.

"For some reason," he elaborated, "I never feel comfortable trying to work out important problems in the office or over lunch. Everything's too confining and formal. I like to negotiate in relaxed surroundings. Somehow a camaraderie develops which enables me, as well as whomever I'm doing business with, to be more frank and direct. I find that I can negotiate in three hours of golf and an hour afterwards what it would take me two weeks to do running around to offices, lawyers, and accountants."

The comfort factor works two ways with respect to strategy. On certain negotiating occasions it will be you who will want to feel comfortable and secure in your surroundings—for whatever psychological or self-image boost it will give you vis-à-vis your opponent.

On other occasions you will find it strategically advantageous to sacrifice your own comfort to ensure that your opponent is comfortable.

With regard to the consideration of one's own comfort, not too long ago a friend of mine—a writer—was summoned by letter for an income tax audit at the nearest IRS office. He had been through such audits before, and each time, after delivering himself and his records to the IRS office, he had come away with an additional tax bill.

"Always piddling amounts," he says. "One year I couldn't substantiate a $40 business expense, and even though I had countless documentation to substantiate every other expense, the auditor slapped me for tax on the $40. Another time an auditor claimed that I deducted too much on a theft loss, and since I couldn't prove what I'd paid for the thing that was stolen, he disallowed it altogether."

My friend claimed that the reason he always got knocked down by the auditors was because he felt intimidated and uncomfortable trying to justify his deductions in the cold, antiseptic cubicles the IRS auditors used to conduct the examinations.

"When I got my last summons, which assigned me a day and time to appear, I wrote back and said that if they wanted to audit my taxes, they would have to do so at my convenience in my home. They kept sending me form letters giving me new dates. I kept writing back saying that I was fully prepared to let them audit me, but that they were going to do it in my home or not at all."

The local office finally acquiesced and requested an appointment at his home. When the auditor arrived, my friend produced the same kind of spotty documentation as in previous years. This time, however, in the psychological comfort of familiar surroundings, he was able to convince the auditor that all his deductions were legitimate. A few weeks later he received a notice of "no change" in his income tax.

The third significance of negotiating location has to do with power—real power. Although I would not expect you to allow yourself to be intimidated into succumbing to "appearances" of opponent power in a negotiation, the conveyance of a sense of real power can be an effective negotiating strategy. And power is often conveyed through the surroundings in which power is exercised.

We all know by now former White House counsel John Dean's rationale for his participation in the Watergate cover-up and other "dirty tricks" of the Nixon administration. Dean claimed that the "awesome power" of the Presidency and its White House milieu overwhelmed him and a number of other "honest men" into checking their ethical principles and morality at the door. . . .

My own offices are set up and decorated in an attractive, open style where visitors walk into a central office that is usually a hub of activity. An international Telex machine chatters in the anteroom; a Xerox machine spews out copies of documents in another; various employees scurry from office to office, while in the background, the soft but incessant ringing of telephones serves as something akin to a symphonic counterpoint that underlines the legitimacy of all the activity.

There is nothing phony or manufactured about the setting. No one wears status-symbol clothes or adorns himself with power-image totems. In short, the setting suggests a highly successful and extremely busy office. What the visitor sees is not illusion but reality.

I realized early on, however, that potential clients are visibly impressed by all the hustle and bustle. Many New York literary agencies—some successful, some not—are run out of their owners' apartments. Others are a warren of ill-lit cubicles in some remote, seedy office building. Still others are sumptuous but solemn sanctorums that resemble mortuaries more than business offices.

I make it a practice to negotiate with prospective clients in my offices because, without any attempt at ostentation or phony power-image building on my part, they can plainly see that we are successful in what we do. I find these surroundings an effective way to communicate to new clients a sense of competence and success that I hope to make them a part of.

All the effects of location, as they relate to negotiating strategy, are largely psychological. There are no hard and fast rules. A particular psychological ploy might work well in one situation, whereas it will fail dismally in another. You might choose to use the tactic of power display against one opponent, hoping to provoke a psychological effect that will redound to your benefit. Use the same tactic with someone else and you're liable to find that your opponent has interpreted your power image as that of a shark and will withdraw from negotiation completely.

The question of *where* to conduct a particular negotiation will often have significant psychological ramifications with respect to your potential for success, but you should not make a fetish of the "psychology" of location. Nor should you become preoccupied with the psychology inherent in any negotiating situation. All negotiation, particularly when it is negotiation aimed at "asking for more and getting it," is fraught with psychological rhythms and counterrhythms. Your goal should be to become sensitive to the rhythms and exploit them when exploitable, not to preinvent psychological ploys and then become tied to them.

In other words, just as you should not be influenced by impressions, surroundings, and other "psychological" devices an opponent might create to intimidate or "psych" you into being more resilient, you should not automatically expect to be able similarly to psych your opponent.

Use location selectively and flexibly. Learn when it is important—either from your point of view or your opponent's—and include it in your strategy. Know when it is unimportant and then dismiss it from your strategy. Above all, don't get locked into psychological presuppositions, whether they relate to location or anything else. Let the psychology flow from the negotiating situation and then selectively take advantage of it.

When

Time is a vital component of strategy. If a negotiation begins too soon, your opponent's expectations may be too high for you to effect any significant compromise or concessions. If it begins too late, your opponent may complete the exchange with someone else.

Bill was a successful jewelry designer. He had zeroed in on a co-op apartment that he wanted and which was owned by an executive of a multinational corporation who told Bill that he expected to be transferred to Europe in another year or so. As it turned out, Bill had to wait two years before this happened and the co-op came up for sale. As soon as it did, he leaped forward to begin negotiations before anyone else had a chance to look at it. The transferred owner, he quickly learned, hoped to get much more for it than it was realistically worth. No matter how Bill tried, he could not budge the owner off his firm price. Bill decided to withdraw from the negotiation.

A few months passed. The owner left for Europe, leaving the sale to a group of brokers. The co-op remained unsold at the price the owner was sticking to. Finally, at the brokers' urging, the owner authorized a few thousand dollars' reduction in the price—barely a scratch on the surface and not enough to reinterest Bill.

Another few months passed and the co-op still remained on the market. When Bill determined that the time was right—when just about every potentially qualified buyer had seen the co-op and had been scared off by the price—he made an offer. His offer was as unrealistically low as the owner's price was high. But he knew that by now the owner was sitting over there in Europe getting discouraged. Bill figured that the owner would welcome any action he could get and at least begin to negotiate seriously.

To Bill's astonishment, the owner accepted his offer without a quibble. It seemed that the timing of the offer had caught the owner at a psychological low point of resistance, and he was happy to get rid of the apartment at almost any price. Bill was aware of the psychological implications of his offer. But the offer was simply a tactic to get the owner moving. Happily, by playing a "waiting game" Bill got the house he wanted, for considerably less than he had originally been willing to pay.

I remember another, similar, case of the benefits of good timing. In this instance it involved a well-known best-selling novelist I had newly agreed to represent.

Henry was a writer of best-sellers long before I met

him. In fact, I began to represent him only a few months earlier, after he grew dissatisfied with his former agent and put out word that he was seeking a new one. I had no trouble in persuading him to sign on exclusively with me for his current and future books. I had a little more difficulty in deciding how to handle the question of the books he had written and published before I became his agent. Most of them had earned a lot of money, and their earning potential was far from exhausted. They were still worth a great deal in future paperback and foreign reprint licenses, as well as movie and television rights.

I deliberated for a long time on how to approach Henry on this question. Theoretically, since he had published the books before he came under my aegis, I should not have expected him to give me a commission on their existing contractual proceeds. I finally settled on proposing that I service his existing contracts for no commission, remitting all the money received from them to him in full, while on any new contracts I negotiated on the old books I would deduct my normal commission.

For some reason—I suppose because I did not want to seem pushy and because I wanted our relationship to have a chance to solidify—I did not immediately raise the point with Henry. I continued to procrastinate for a few more weeks, during which time I negotiated two very favorable contracts for him on new books. Then, one day, to my great surprise, he called and asked me to represent all his previous books, service the existing contracts, and charge a commission on all income, old and new.

Time had played into my hands. By not beginning the negotiation prematurely, I had gotten all that I wanted and more.

It is generally true in all negotiating situations that the passage of time makes opponents willing to be more flexible in the concessions they make. Somehow, one's expectations decline when time passes without any positive action. This is as true in the rest of life's endeavors as it is in negotiation.

Occasionally in negotiating, lowered expectations come about because we are soliciting other offers simultaneously, and the information provided by those offers over a period of time makes us more certain of the realistically available goal ranges. In other cases, it is simply because as time goes on and we bargain back and forth, we begin to realize that the upper ranges of our goal will not be attainable. In still other cases, it may be the accumulation of common ground between our opponent and us that makes us more flexible.

Time and timing, however, are tricky categories. Time can work against you just as easily as it can work for you. In some negotiations, it is best to work for the quickest conclusion possible so that your opponent won't have time to reflect on the concessions you've extracted from him or her. In others, it is best to proceed more cautiously, giving your opponent time to reflect.

There are no hard and fast rules about time except this: Learn to be acutely aware of the importance of the time and timing factors in any negotiation, since such awareness can play a significant role in helping you to "ask for more and get it."

Be aware always that your opponent may be using time or various aspects of timing in his or her approaches to you. Say you've advertised your car for sale in the papers at a certain price, have run the ad for four weeks, but still haven't sold the car. One day you receive a call from someone who says he's just seen the ad and he's interested. It is in your interest to be sure, if you can, that he actually just saw the ad, that he had not seen it for four weeks running and decided that, since you hadn't sold it, the time was ripe to contact you with a low offer.

Timing in any negotiation is a richly variegated asset

when you know how to use it, and a potential time bomb when you are not attuned to it.

Recently, after months of difficult negotiation for a particular group of properties I very much wanted, it came time to set up a meeting to go over the final points of the purchase contract and sign the final agreements. The seller, an older man, had asked my attorney to set the closing early in the day. Because of his need to be in court most mornings, my attorney finally set a twelve o'clock meeting.

The results were disastrous. The meeting had gone on six hours and the seller had grown weary. We were close to signing, but literally one minor point out of a thousand remained to be discussed. An associate of mine took up discussion of the point and ended up pushing the seller too far. Almost imperceptibly, the seller reached out for the thick file of contracts on the conference table, slipped them into his briefcase, and walked out of the meeting. At first we thought he was on the way to the men's room, but when he took his coat, I knew that six months of work and an important deal to me had melted before my very eyes.

I'm convinced that had the point been raised earlier in the negotiation, it would have been settled without a thought. But my associate's timing was ill-advised; the seller was just too tired to cope with another barrage of back-and-forth discussion.

The deal was closed two months later, but at a $50,000 increase in price. The seller had taken the weekend after he walked out of the unsuccessful contract meeting to rethink the deal and the price. There is no question in my mind that had my associate been sensitive to the timing issue, the deal would have closed at the original price without a question. His timing was off by minutes, but it cost me $50,000.

Part Five
TACTICS

Chapter 11

Conflict Avoidance

There are two general classes of tactics that one can employ to bring about a favorable negotiation. The first relates to practically all negotiations and may be all that is needed to ease a simple negotiation to a favorable conclusion.

The second class relates to tougher and more complex negotiations and should be used selectively, as the progress of each individual negotiation requires.

I call the first class "conflict avoidance tactics." It is based on two simple concepts: (1) *revealing goal priorities* and (2) *positioning for easy acceptance.* In both cases, the tactics involve reducing the potential conflict that a particular goal objective will cause your opponent and thereby ensuring his acceptance of your goal objectives and minimizing his demands for counterbalancing concessions.

Revealing Goal Priorities

Generally, a negotiation will begin with the most important objectives first and proceed from there to the less important. The most obvious reason for this derives from the conventional rituals of negotiation. That is, the parties will not want to spend time discussing secondary issues until they are convinced that an agreement on the primary issues is possible.

This is a linear approach to negotiation which is often all that is needed to conclude a simple negotiation. However, when you are using negotiation to "ask for more and get it," the customary linear approach should be abandoned. You should decide the order of issues to be discussed, based on your strategic perceptions of the possible linkages and other concession-inducing possibilities inherent in the negotiating encounter (your opponent's psychology, his or her criteria and rationales, his or her needs, his or her enthusiasm, etc.), and then order the issues accordingly.

EXAMPLE:

You decide to sell your house. You begin negotiations with a potential buyer. You learn from your preliminary criteria discussions that he is extremely pleased with the house, that he needs to acquire a house as quickly as possible because he has been transferred from another part of the country and cannot have his family join him until he has obtained living accommodations, and that his financial background qualifies him to pay the price you are asking. The only trouble is that he has indicated misgivings about your price; he has said, "Frankly, I was really thinking of something in a range about $10,000 less than you're asking."

If you were an unskilled or tactically unprepared

negotiator, you would most likely proceed to immediately "attack" the question of price, your primary goal and probably his. This would be a mistake. The tactically skilled seller-negotiator would manipulate the discussion around the price issue. He would focus the beginning stages of the negotiation on all the positive factors in the potential buyer's mind—those things that have obviously provoked his enthusiasm for the house. These may include move-in time, the house's style, number of rooms, location, various conveniences, fashionable postal address (often an important psychological factor), and so on. These may be secondary goals on the part of the buyer, but taken together they might outweigh his primary price goal. By getting agreement on these secondary goals, the experienced negotiator will more often than not succeed in obtaining a more advantageous agreement on price.

The decision about whether to present a particular goal as primary or secondary, as essential or nonessential, can be a crucial one in terms of tactics. Often we may have a goal that is essential, but that is not obvious as such to our opponent.

In the above example, an additional essential goal of yours might be to sell the house as quickly as possible because you've already put a down payment on another one and you desperately need the proceeds from the first house to close the deal on the second. If your opponent were to know this, he would be in a much better position to force you into a concession on your price goal. Obviously, you should not let him know this until the latter stages of the negotiation. At that time, if you're only a hair's breadth away from an agreement and need just one final inducement to bring your opponent around, you might introduce your hidden primary goal. "Look," you might say, "I haven't mentioned this before, but I'd like to get out of here as soon as possible. If you agree to everything else and we can conclude a deal right now, I'll throw in the washer and drier in the basement for nothing."

By introducing hidden essential goals later in a negotiation, at the time your nonessential goals are being agreed upon or your criteria are being met, you are in a good position to win the objective without being obliged to make counterbalancing primary-goal compromises.

Similarly, it is possible to win secondary goal concessions from your opponent by introducing those goals into the negotiation at a time when he or she is not prepared for secondary objectives.

An opponent will often concede one or more secondary goals as an opening concession designed to get the negotiations started. Of course, you can do the same thing.

Again, using the above house negotiation example, you might say at the outset, when the potential buyer expresses hesitation about your price, "Look, normally it is your responsibility as the buyer to pay for the recording fees and the tax stamps. As a gesture of good will, I will take over that responsibility, if we can make progress on the other items."

Be careful, however, when you use opening concessions as a tactic, for they may in the long run be unduly costly. Your concession of a minor value may encourage your opponent to believe that he can press for greater concessions on the next goal objective to be discussed.

This tactic, in short, can backfire on you, whether you are the buyer or the seller. Suppose you are looking for a house and have found one you would really like to buy. You are meeting with the owner and are about to make an offer.

The property includes a vast lawn area (one of the features you like most), and you have seen a special mowing machine in the garage that is probably worth $1,000. You begin the discussion by saying that you are interested in the house, but the asking price is more than you wish to pay. Because of the large amount of lawn, you would only consider making an offer if the seller agrees to include the mower in the sale.

The owner will probably agree to include the mower. But you will have tipped the tenor of the negotiation away from yourself with this opening, for the owner, having indicated his willingness to concede on a secondary point, will be in a better position to sustain his primary point—the price of the house. Had you begun with a strong rationale-shaped attack on the price of the house, you might have been able to obtain a concession worth many times the value of the mower. By demanding and accepting the negotiation's first concession, a minor one, for yourself, you have weakened your position on the major concession you desire.

Lastly, a reminder that, as we discussed in Chapter 6, about common ground, whenever an opponent's goal concession is not attainable during the early stages of a negotiation, no matter how major or minor the objective is, it would be an effective tactic to suggest to your opponent that further discussion of the issue be postponed. Invariably, assuming that you do not reach an impasse on too many issues, compromises will be possible later on as a result of the common ground that has been established on other objectives.

Positioning for Easy Acceptance

Positioning for easy acceptance is the tactic of structuring a goal so that your opponent can agree to it with the least *apparent* sacrifice on his or her part.

Goal concessions are often resisted because they are structured or positioned in such a way as to cause the opponent's embarrassment and loss of prestige or self-esteem or to demand of the opponent a radical change in his criteria. In my experience, the proper structuring and positioning of

goal objectives is one of the most powerful tools of the negotiator. I have already given you several examples of this tactic, such as my negotiation with Lewis the architect over the
question of his hourly fee. Let us look at one or two others.

EXAMPLE:

You are a woman with two minor children, involved in a separation-divorce negotiation with your
soon-to-be-ex. You are conducting the negotiation
through your attorney, but you (as you always should
with shields) have the final authority on compromises
and concessions.

You know that your demands for alimony and
child support will be vigorously resisted by your husband, thereby prolonging your unwanted marriage. Yet
you dare not let him off the hook by not asking for
what you believe are your and your children's rightful
due.

Your money demands are based on your standard
of living and your husband's salary (these are the two
basic concepts the courts follow when deciding on
alimony and child support): You want $200 a week for
yourself and $50 a week for each of your children, for
a total of $300 a week.

Your husband replies that this is impossible, since
he makes at his present job only $400. It means that he
will have only $100 a week to live on, which will pre-
vent him from being able to enjoy anything more than
a subsistence existence.

Your reply is that you know and he knows that he
is due in another year or so for a promotion to another
job which will raise his salary to $750 a week. He has
also started a side business which earns him an additional $50 a week and might produce much more in the
future, and he has investments that yield about $30 a
week in dividend income.

At this point your lawyer might suggest that you restructure or reposition your financial demands in such a way as to encourage your husband's acceptance of them. One way to do this would be, instead of demanding a flat amount, to propose a percentage formula based on your husband's gross income. That is, up to a certain amount of his yearly income, he would be obliged to pay a percentage equivalent to say, $200 a week. If his gross income in a given year exceeds that amount up to a certain figure, the percentage formula will require him to pay an additional $100 a week. And if it goes beyond that figure, he will be required to pay additional weekly sums.

In this way, you and your children are guaranteed a reasonable amount at the beginning. Because of your anticipation of your husband's future financial improvement, moreover, you can be sure that you will get your additional share of whatever prosperity he enjoys.

More likely than not, your husband would accept such a proposal, for it gives him a little more breathing room and, in a sense, provides the encouragement to increase his income. The more he can make, according to the percentage formula, the more he will have to pay. But as his income goes up, the differential between what he pays and what he keeps goes down. In other words, the more money he earns, the more he gets to keep, despite the fact that you are well provided for.

EXAMPLE:

I recently had a negotiation with the trustee for a family trust that held a second mortgage on a property I was buying as a result of a foreclosure by the bank which held the first mortgage. The trust's mortgage, which had a face value of $50,000, was practically worthless. I offered the trust a nominal fee of $2,000 to avoid the legal costs of having to foreclose their position in the property. The trustee I was dealing with indicated to me that it would be very difficult for him to accept my offer since it would mean admitting to the other trustees that this asset had declined in value by $48,000. He suggested that I offer him no money, but agree to pay the entire $50,000 contingent on some future eventuality, even if that eventuality was remote and unlikely (such as my sale of the property at five times what I paid for it within three years). That way, he would not have to acknowledge overtly the worthlessness of the mortgage to his cotrustees.

Simply by restructuring my objective for my opponent's easy acceptance, I was able to get what I wanted for less than I had been prepared to pay.

EXAMPLE:

Frank had been working as an agent in my literary agency for less than a year. I had started him at a salary of $10,000 and increased him to $12,000 after six months. He was easily my most productive agent, outselling his five counterparts, who had all been with me for five years or more, two to one.

With the end of his first year approaching, Frank sought me out to negotiate another raise. As part of his leverage he used the fact that he had been offered a job at another agency at a large increase in salary. He also pointed out his productivity factor as compared to my other five agents.

I did not want to lose Frank. But the raise he was seeking would have put him well above the other agents, who, while they were selling less, had been loyal to me and valuable to the agency over the years. I couldn't accede to Frank's salary demand without incurring a morale problem with my other agents.

As an alternative, I suggested a commission-bonus arrangement that would effectively increase his income to the point he was requesting, as long as he continued to produce, but would not get me in trouble with my other employees. If they sold as much, they would earn as much. On the other hand, they would not be demoralized by lower salaries despite their seniority. Frank accepted this alternative.

I gave Frank what he wanted, but made the conditions such that I was not forced to put myself in a compromised position, which my agreement to the original structuring of his goals would have resulted in. In a sense I repositioned his goals for him so that they were easily acceptable to all concerned.

When negotiating objectives, always be sensitive to the nonfinancial and nonmaterial costs to your opponent of a concession. As much as possible be flexible and inventive in the ways in which you pursue goals. The less the *apparent* cost to your opponent (regardless of the reality), the greater will be your ability to achieve a favorable concession or compromise. Always be on the lookout for such opportunities, and then make the tactical best of them.

Chapter 12

Basic Negotiating Tactics

In this chapter I will discuss the twelve most effective tactics that you can employ in a negotiation. These tactics and an infinite number of variations of them, along with other less important tactics that I do not describe, comprise the essence of the negotiating process. With an awareness of these twelve vital tactics, you will have a solid basis from which to pursue effective and imaginative negotiations.

I call these tactics "negotiating tactics" since they involve an overt decision on your part to use one or more of them as a way to manage and direct a given negotiation to a desired end. They are the means you will use to increase the effectiveness of your criteria, rationales, and counter-rationales so that you can achieve maximum positioning.

Tactics, I might caution, should not be thought of as separate entities to be applied one after the other, as in, "First I'll try this, then this, then this, until I hit upon the right tactic." Such an approach is akin to how an inexpe-

rienced prizefighter uses his punches—first a jab, then a
hook, followed by a cross, and so on. The skilled fighter
avoids the plodding punch-by-punch approach and uses
combinations of punches—jab-jab-uppercut-hook, jab-upper-
cut-cross, hook-uppercut-jab-cross—in a continuous flow of
motion.

1. "Market Tactics," or Simultaneous Negotiations

In most of the negotiations we have discussed there
have been usually just two parties. Each exchanges something he owns or controls for something he wants or needs.
Exactly how much is given up or taken is decided by
agreement after discussion between the parties. Each makes
such concessions as he feels are warranted by his assessment
of the value of the exchange.

My willingness to trade for a given item is based primarily on my need for the item. If my need is great, my willingness to sacrifice for it will be correspondingly great. If my
need is minimal, my willingness to make extreme concessions
will be equally minimal. However, exchanges in which your
subjective need for a given item determines its value to you
will only be one type of negotiation you will encounter. A
market tactic, or simultaneous negotiation, will often be
employed by your opponent to influence or determine the
basis on which an exchange can be carried off.

The most common example of a market tactic, or simultaneous negotiation, is the auction. A given exchange is
offered to a group of people simultaneously, and each is
asked to reveal the value of the exchange by bidding on the
item being offered. I was recently at a farm auction where a
practically new refrigerator was being offered for sale. The
day before the auction I approached the farmer privately
and asked if he would take $100 for it. I thought my offer
was fair (a new model of the same refrigerator sold for

$150), but the farmer refused. The next day the refrigerator went for $135. When I asked the successful bidder why he was willing to pay a price that was only $15 less than that of a new model, he told me that his own refrigerator had conked out on him that morning and that by acquiring this refrigerator he would be able to save $75 worth of food from spoiling. His subjective emergency need made the refrigerator worth a great deal more to him than to me. A market tactic had enabled the farmer to find the person willing to pay the most for the item he was offering.

Like so many things in life, market tactics also have a negative side. The bidding for the refrigerator had begun at $50, and the only two bidders beyond $70 were me and the eventual buyer. If his refrigerator had not broken down that morning, he would not have been at the auction. The refrigerator would then have been mine for $75, or $25 less than I had offered the farmer for it the day before.

By exposing a given exchange to competitive bidding, the seller has decided to use "comparative value" as the ultimate rationale for the price at which he expects the exchange to be consummated. He has, in effect, placed all other rationales in subordinate positions and offered to consummate the exchange according to a set of goal compromises to be determined by the "relatives offers" of all the potential purchasers he can attract or interest in the exchange.

Prospective buyers will make their offers based on what other prospective buyers have offered, up to the maximum value they attribute to the item being exchanged. The advantage to you of this type of negotiation is that you, as seller, will not be unduly influenced by the rationales and values of a particular purchaser, but will benefit from a broader sample of market value input.

On the other hand, there is a counterbalancing disadvantage. A purchaser who may attribute a high maximum value to a particular exchange will only offer a portion of that value if there is no bidder with a competitive and equal maximum valuation.

In the simplest form of auction, the person offering the exchange agrees to complete it with whoever offers the best terms, even if those terms are below his minimum goal objectives. In a sense, the person offering the exchange on a bid basis gives up his right to negotiate on any rationale other than comparative value. His own sense of value, or other rationales, must be surrendered to those of the market place. Goal compromises are no longer struck between seller and buyer based on their respective rationales and counter-rationales. Rather, they are settled by comparative value as determined between competing buyers.

EXAMPLE:

I recently agreed to represent the author of a book applying behaviorist psychological techniques to a particular area of human interchange. I thought the manuscript to be a very good and salable project and offered it to about ten publishers. I asked each publisher to make a first bid by the following Tuesday and said I would allow bidding to continue through the end of that week.

A few days after I distributed material on the proposed book, one of the publishers I sent it to called me up and offered to buy it for $20,000 if he could close the deal then and there. I refused, reminding him that it was on simultaneous offer to several publishers with an auction closing scheduled for the following week.

By the agreed-upon Tuesday, I had received four offers—two for $7,500, one for $12,500 and one for $15,000. The publisher who had originally offered $20,000 made his first offer under the auction arrangement at $12,500, hoping that no other publisher would offer a higher amount and that, under the auction arrangement, he could secure the book for a lower amount that he had already indicated he felt the book was worth.

Fortunately, I had an offer of $15,000 and could turn down the first publisher's bid of $12,500. Soon, one of the publishers who had bid $7,500 jumped his bid to $17,500; the auction got underway, with the various publishers bidding the final price up to $32,500.

In this example, the auction technique worked. But I recall another instance in which, under similar circumstances, a friend was forced to sell a valuable art object for considerably less than a negotiated offer would have brought him.

EXAMPLE:

Carl had inherited a Chinese vase from his mother. He knew it was valuable but didn't know exactly how much it was worth. Because he wanted to purchase a country home Carl decided to sell it and asked me for the name of a reputable dealer. I referred him to someone I knew who was honest and who held regular auctions of fine antique porcelains and other art objects.

The dealer appraised the vase at $8,500 and offered to place it up for sale at his next auction. A few days before the sale, the dealer called Carl, indicated that a private party had offered $7,500 for the vase, and asked whether Carl wanted to consider the offer. The dealer told Carl that his appraisal was only an estimate and that the price at auction could easily be substantially less, or more. Carl decided to take a chance on the auction.

At the auction the opening bidder was the same party who had offered $7,500 privately to the dealer. His opening bid was $6,000. Unfortunately for Carl, there were no other bidders and the sale was consummated at a price 20 per cent less than that which he had been offered only a few days before.

Whether or not a negotiation is formally called a "simultaneous negotiation," there is an element of comparative value in all exchanges. This is expressed by the tacit assumption ever present but rarely explicitly stated, that if your opponent does not offer suitable goal compromises there are others who will. Of course, in the one-on-one negotiation, there is a third possibility. It is that if a suitable offer is not made you will simply not enter into the anticipated exchange with anyone.

In a sense, reflecting this alternative, simultaneous negotiations often occur in much more complex and modified forms than the explicit, totally market-controlled form described in our first examples. Many auctions, for instance, require at least three bids before the seller is required to accept the highest offer. Often the first bid's acceptance is at the discretion of the auctioneer, thus preventing the forced sale of an item at a ridiculously low price.

The modified forms of simultaneous negotiation are usually the most advantageous, since they can utilize the rationale of comparative value and at the same time involve many of the processes and downside protections of a one-on-one negotiation.

There is an almost endless variety of modifications that can be applied to the tactic of simultaneous negotiation in its pure form, but most of them usually involve a "minimum valuation" technique.

EXAMPLE:

Henry decides to sell 100 shares of General Motors stock. He gives an order to his stockbroker to sell the stock at the market price (the last quotation was 51½), but at not less than $51 per share.

Henry's stockbroker will offer his shares at an "ask" price relative to the last market trade, but Henry's minimum price will protect him from the stock being sold at a "bid" price below his minimum price objective.

At the end of the day Henry's stockbroker calls to tell him that the stock closed at 50¼ and that there were no buyers at his minimum price of 51. Perhaps tomorrow the price will rise and Henry will get his minimum price accepted.

EXAMPLE:

The following ad appeared in the used-car classified section of the New York *Times*:

> Toyota, 1975 fastback; 23,000
> miles; excellent condition;
> white interior w/sun roof:
> best offer over $2,000. Call
> Tom 371–6453

I called Tom and asked him what he meant by "best offer over $2,000." Tom said that I should come and look at the car, give him my best offer over $2,000, and he would let me know by the end of the week whether it was acceptable. His plan was to collect offers until Friday afternoon and then accept the best one.

I went to Tom's house, examined the car, and left a bid of $2,250. At the end of the week Tom called me to say the car was mine since the next highest offer was only $2,100.

In my experience, one of the most effective modifications of the tactic of simultaneous negotiation is an exchange made on a "best offer" basis. Much as in the ad for the Toyota, each party is given an opportunity to make his highest offer, knowing that other purchasers will be doing the same but without knowing exactly what their offers will be. In this situation, a prospective purchaser will usually bid his maximum valuation since he will be concerned that another higher offer will be made and that he will lose the opportunity to enter into the exchange on what otherwise would have been acceptable terms.

EXAMPLE:

I sent a proposal for a book on child care to three publishers. The first publisher called me up and offered $7,500. The second publisher, very enthusiastic about the project, called and asked whether he and the other publishers could bid openly in an auction for the book since he didn't want to chance losing it because of too low a "best offer."

I declined and said that I would prefer it if both he and the third publisher simply made their best offer. The third publisher made his offer, which was $15,000. The second publisher, not knowing what his competitors were willing to pay but very much wanting the book, offered his maximum valuation—$50,000. This very handsome offer was much more than he would have offered had he been bidding against the publisher who he knew had offered only $15,000. Needless to say, I was glad I had insisted on the "best offer" basis rather than agreeing to an auction.

A common defensive tactic used in auctions is the making of a "pre-emptive bid." In this situation an offerer makes a bid which is considerably higher than the current level of bids, but requires the seller to accept or reject the bid without going back to any of the other bidders and using it as a basis for soliciting still higher competitive bids.

EXAMPLE:

I recently participated in the bidding for a Manhattan office building which had been taken over in foreclosure proceedings by a large New York bank. The bank offered the property for $1,500,000 but indicated that it would might consider bids as low as $1,200,000. The bank said that it would consider offers for a two-week period and then make a deal with the highest bidder. I was very interested in the property and believed that other buyers would be too. I was prepared to pay even more than the $1,200,000 the bank had indicated was acceptable and suspected that competitive offers might push the price even higher. I told the bank that I wanted the property and was willing to make a substantial offer, provided that the bank agreed to accept or reject it without waiting until the end of the two-week period.

I made a "pre-emptive offer" of $1,300,000 but with the provision that it be accepted or rejected within twenty-four hours without reference to any other bids. It was accepted. I had pre-empted all other potential bidders by making a comparatively high initial bid.

In summary, simultaneous negotiation can be one of the most useful tactics available to ensure maximum goal achievement. However, in using this tactic, it is essential to understand that it can backfire and result in goal compromises substantially below their maximum potential, particularly if you do not have enough potential bidders to create a competitive market for the exchange in question.

2. *Precedents*

In many negotiating situations, the concern of the respective parties over the precedent-setting nature of particular goal concessions will be a substantial factor in the parties' willingness to make the concessions. An expression often heard is, "But if I do that for you, I'll have to do it for everybody." The precedent-setting nature of a goal concession is a legitimate concern of the parties to a negotiation and must be taken into account. Thus, it is important that you recognize any precedence factors that may reside in the concessions you are seeking. Many times your opponent will not let you know that his resistance to a concession is based on his fear of the precedent such a concession might establish. When faced with firm "precedent resistance," you should think about structuring alternative goal-compromise requests so that you can still obtain the desired concession without creating an unacceptable precedent in the mind of your opponent.

EXAMPLE:

Max is a key worker in a small office of fifteen employees and wishes to take some night courses to widen his skills and expand his future employment possibilities. He has not had a raise in two years and thinks he's overdue for one. Max goes to the boss and makes his request. The boss tells him that business has not been good, and because of that no one has had a raise— even he has taken a cut in salary. If he gives Max a raise, it would be unfair to the others in the office, some of whom are senior to Max in employment. By giving Max a raise he would be setting a precedent by which he would be required to raise all the other employees, or else. And if he did that, the company might not survive the estimated $30,000 increase in its payroll.

Max knows that his job is vital to the firm, that he would have no trouble finding employment elsewhere at a probable increase in salary, and that the firm would be highly inconvenienced by having to break in someone else to take his place. He enjoys the work environment of his present job, however, and wishes to avoid looking for a new one. Max decides to restructure his raise request. He agrees to postpone action on his raise request for six months, or until business takes an upturn, whichever comes first. He asks instead that he be compensated in another way. He would like an immediate lump-sum bonus as a reward for staying on the job and would like the company to pay the tuition for his additional night schooling. Max assures the boss that he will keep confidential whatever arrangement the two of them arrive at.

Max's boss now has a workable alternative. Having weighed Max's value to the firm and being offered a way to avoid setting an unwanted precedent, Max's boss agrees to a lump-sum payment and tuition reimbursement.

Equally troublesome as one-time precedents are concession requests that occur in negotiations which may be interpreted as setting precedents for future dealings with the same opponent. In my businesses, I often deal with the same people on a continuing basis. I recently entered into a real estate venture, for instance, with a financial partner with whom I expect to have future partnership arrangements. In general, I felt that the terms we negotiated with respect to our initial venture were fair. Nevertheless, one term—a special commission to the partner's wife—was in my view onerous. I finally consented to it because I wanted to conclude my first agreement with this new partner. But I was concerned that it might become a precedent for future deals and that I would be expected to agree to such a commission every time we entered into a coventure. Therefore, when agreeing to it in the first instance, I went to great pains to emphasize that I was doing so reluctantly and only as a one-time gesture of good will to my new partner. I made it clear that such requests would not be acceptable in future dealings.

Denying the precedent-setting nature of a concession will not leave you entirely free from future demands for such concessions, but it will at least put you on record with some defense. I fully expect my partner to raise the commission-to-his-wife question again on our next deal. I will firmly resist it, but in reality I expect that my ultimate decision will hinge on the mix of other goal concessions and on whether I feel the exchange in its entirety is beneficial to me or not.

One last point about precedents. The precedent argument is often used all too easily, particularly by institutions and bureaucracies. You will frequently hear such disclaimers as "I'm sorry, but your request is against the company's policy" or "That's just not the way we do things around here." By offering alternative goal-concession structures, you will gain an effective means of testing the validity of your opponent's precedent rationale. You will frequently discover that although your opponent is unwilling to do something one way, he will be willing to do practically the same thing in another.

If it is you who decide to resort to the precedent argument to resist a concession request, make sure you are prepared for alternative proposals designed to obtain the same concession.

3. How "No" Is "No"—Winning Through Persistence

Frequently the first reaction of people to an idea or proposal that is new or alien to them is "No." However, despite such an initial rejection the potential for eventual acceptance or acquiescence may well remain. When the point is pressed or framed in a slightly different way, the opponent's response may totally contradict his first reaction.

One often experiences immediate and outright "No" reactions to proposals made to enter into exchanges, particularly when the person to whom the proposal is made is not expecting it. People often react negatively simply because they don't want to appear too eager to enter into the exchange or because they are uncertain and want time to think the proposal over.

EXAMPLE:

　　　Elizabeth was an attractive young attorney working in a large, established midtown law firm. In the course of negotiating a new recording contract for one of the firm's clients, she was introduced to Kit, a vice-president of the record company. After a long afternoon of hard negotiating, Kit, Elizabeth, another lawyer from her firm, and the client went to dinner.

　　　The next day, Thursday, Kit called her. Admitting that it might be excessively forward of him, and on short notice, he nevertheless suggested that she join him for a weekend of skiing in Colorado. Elizabeth had been very attracted to Kit during dinner and was tempted to go. But she also felt a conflict professionally and personally. Would it affect their business relationship and her position at the firm? And on the personal level, she wasn't used to running off to spend weekends with strange men.

　　　"That's very kind of you, Kit, but I'm afraid I couldn't possibly go." After she hung up, she began to regret her decision.

　　　Fortunately, seconds later, the phone rang again. It was Kit. "Why not, why can't you go? I think you should reconsider. We'll have a terrific time. And don't worry about our business relationship, we'll keep that

separate." This time she accepted—they had a lovely
trip and it was the beginning of a great romance.

The initial rejection of a proposal will not always be
what it appears to be, and persistence, whatever form it
might take, can often reverse it. This phenomenon is extremely important to keep in mind during any negotiation.
"No" is a reaction, not a concept. The person who reacts
negatively to your request may simply need time to evaluate
it; having gathered together the various underlying factors
(as he sees them) he may still conclude that your offer or
request is unacceptable. By presenting these factors in a
different light and showing your opponent that a particular
concession might be warranted after all, *however,* you may
change his "No" reaction to a "Yes."

When trying to entice a potential opponent into a negotiation, never hesitate to persist with either words or actions.
And when you are in the midst of a negotiation and meet resistance, never hesitate to reapproach old ground once,
twice, or as many times as it takes to enlighten your opponent to the virtues of acceptance or compromise.

EXAMPLE:

I recently purchased a group of properties that I
had been pursuing for over five years. The first time I
heard about them, I called the broker and told him I
was interested. When we arrived at the buildings to inspect them, the superintendent refused to show us
around claiming they were not for sale. The broker
insisted they were and and placed a call to the owner in
the super's presence. To the broker's chagrin the owner
announced that he had just taken them off the market.

Four years later I heard the properties were again
for sale. I called the broker and set a date to inspect
them. *Déjà vu*—when we arrived at the properties the

same super once more announced that the properties were not for sale and said that he would not show them to us. Again the broker placed a call to the owner who again said he had just taken them off the market.

I wanted the buildings badly enough to take drastic action. I decided to make a blind bid without having inspected them, in the hope that my offer would force the owner to take my interest seriously and abandon his mysterious vacillation.

My strategy worked. Negotiations ensued and two months later the buildings were mine. The problem as it turned out had been that the super, who had worked for the owner for twenty-five years was against the sale. The owner had considered the super a personal friend and had suffered some conflict about whether to sell the properties or not. It required the overt act of a third party to overcome his reluctance.

In addition to being a reaction, "No" is also often used as a ploy in the "reluctant seller/buyer" routine.

When negotiating, it is frequently useful for you to start off with a calculatedly negative approach and then modify your stance in a more positive direction from there. You may indeed be enthusiastic to conclude an exchange. But there is no reason to show your enthusiasm. By your being negative at the outset, each time you modify your position you appear to be making a concession or compromise. Your opponent's concession requests will be much less demanding in the face of your apparent attitude toward the negotiation. Hence the concessions you *do* make will be less to your disadvantage than they might otherwise be.

I have a friend who is a classic example of the "reluctant seller." He always starts out by saying "No" to any new idea or business proposal that is brought to him. However, he always indicates that he would not be averse to further information so that he can "examine the matter from all sides." This usually puts him in the position of reluctant seller and forces his opponent to come forward with his very best terms, holding nothing back, in order to ignite my friend's interest.

EXAMPLE:

Chris had wanted nothing more than to sell his apple crop to one buyer so that he would not have to worry about marketing his apples into the late fall and could devote the time saved to finishing the book he was working on. However, when the apple buyer from a large chain offered him $3.75 per bushel, instead of jumping at the near-record price he told the buyer that he wanted to think about it for a few days. In reality, he couldn't have been more willing to sell at the quoted price, which was higher than he had been expecting.

The buyer, anxious to secure Chris's prime apples for his stores, offered to increase the price to $4.00 if they could close the deal immediately. Chris, ever the long-shot player, told the buyer he'd be more inclined to deal if the price was $4.25. The buyer hesitated but then extended his hand. Chris made the best crop sale of his farming career.

The line between "No" and "Yes" is often a very thin one. Never accept "Never" as a response. Almost every "No" is itself a negotiable position. Given the right rationales, the right counterbalancing concessions, most "Noes" can be turned into "Yesses" or at least "Maybes." The "No" that appears so considered and definite might really represent nothing more than an opponent's way out of an illusory conflict. By probing the reasons for a person's negative response, you may find more often than not that he can be won over to the point of acceding to your objective.

4. The Contract Tactic

There is an old saying, "A man's word is his bond." Verbal agreements are fine for simple exchanges and legally binding, as far as they go. However, more complex exchanges are usually reflected in a written agreement; indeed, most exchanges require a contract under the so-called statute of frauds.

In New York State the statute of frauds says that an agreement for value in excess of $500 or for an obligation to be performed later than one year from the date of the agreement must be in writing or it is unenforceable. Negotiations which will eventually be recorded in a written contract often take place in two stages. The first stage comprises the negotiations and agreements reached prior to the writing of the formal contract. These negotiations will usually resolve the most substantive goal objectives involved in the exchange. Many objectives, however, will not be discussed until the contracts are drawn. Eventually, the contract itself will become part of the agenda for the second stage of the negotiations. The previously undiscussed provisions of the contract and reactions to them will become future negotiating points.

EXAMPLE:

Nikki negotiated with a carpenter to build an addition to her house and reached a verbal agreement with him on the substantive points—price, time limits, cleanup and the like. Following this, Nikki asked her lawyer to prepare a written contract for the work to be performed based on her preliminary discussions with the carpenter.

When Nikki got a draft of the contract from her lawyer, it included several provisions which Nikki thought desirable, but which she had not discussed with the carpenter. The additional provisions included a reduction in price (daily penalties) against any time overrun on the part of the carpenter, a requirement that the carpenter take out special liability insurance, and a requirement that the carpenter "restore to the original" any damage to the house or landscaping, specifically to Nikki's prize rose bed which was right next to the area in which the extension was being built.

After reading the contract, the carpenter said he was agreeable to the additional points subject to certain modifications. He asked that the time overrun provision have a phrase added absolving him of any responsibility for delays caused by weather or by supply shortages which he could not control. In addition he asked that Nikki build a temporary fence around her garden to protect it during construction. Lastly, he asked Nikki to pay for one half the cost of the special liability insurance which he had not taken into account when he prepared his bid.

Nikki agreed to all his counterpoints and they signed the contract. The extension was built on schedule, and the only casualty was a light fixture on the patio which the carpenter promptly replaced.

In this way, the written contract itself becomes a subject of the negotiation. And not just its provisions, but its language as well. This is especially important, for the nuances of wording can completely change the legal meaning of a contract provision.

One of the questions which invariably presents itself whenever a written contract itself is involved in a negotiation, is whether you should consult a lawyer or not. There is no easy answer. If lawyers were not so expensive, it would clearly be to your advantage to do so. But their cost must be taken into account. (Is it worth a $75 legal bill to review a $350 contract?) The answer depends on whether the contract is in an area (type of exchange) you are familiar with, whether there is a potential for hidden liabilities which may far exceed the face value of the contract, and finally how reliable the person with whom you are entering into the exchange is. There is an old axiom among lawyers and experienced businessmen that "a written contract is only as good as the person who signs it." Because of the high expense and inconvenience of litigation, what good is it to have a contract that provides X, Y, and Z, if the parties do not fulfill their obligations. Would Nikki have taken the carpenter to court if he refused to replace the light fixture he had broken? Probably not.

A contract draft usually establishes the agenda for a contract negotiation, and because of the subtleties of contract language, it is often a distinct advantage for *you* to draw up or prepare the contract rather than let your opponent do so. This is true even though certain provisions and modes of language may subsequently be amended through further negotiation. In addition, it usually puts the side that drafts the agreement on the offensive and the opponent on the defensive. Even in less important negotiations you should, when possible, persuade your opponent to let you prepare the contract draft. Your opponent may have verbally agreed to A, B, and C. When you write these agreements down, you may *phrase* them as A_1, B_3, and C_2. That is, they may still be essentially what your opponent agreed to, but couched in terms that are more favorable to yourself. Your opponent may object to some of the ways in which prior verbal agreements have been defined, and his objections will then become subjects of further negotiation. But by using the contract or "draft of agreement" in this way, you give yourself a tactical advantage by which you can gain objectives, either on the uncontested contract provisions or through favorable concessions on the disputed goal agreements or through as yet undiscussed or unresolved goals.

EXAMPLE:

A client of mine, Steven Black, had agreed to collaborate with a major sports figure on his autobiography. They had agreed to split all earnings from the book fifty-fifty. When Steven called to tell me about the arrangement, he mentioned that his coauthor, Bill, had suggested that he have his manager draw up a collaboration agreement. I told Steven that I would rather prepare the collaboration agreement myself because there were a number of important issues to be resolved and I felt the best way to introduce them into the negotiation was through a "draft contract."

I prepared an agreement that provided for an equal sharing of earnings, but which had the following additional important provisions:

1. All Steven's travel expenses while on the road with Bill would be taken off the top. (Bill's expenses were paid by the team, but Steven would have had to pay his own from his share of the earnings if I had not specified otherwise.)
2. All editorial decisions should be totally Steven's.
3. All licenses would be subject to both parties' mutual approval, except that a predetermined third party was named to resolve any conflicts.

When Steven saw the agreement, he was a little concerned that Bill might be put off by the additional provisions but agreed that I should proceed to negotiate the points. I submitted the proposed contract to Bill's manager, who was agreeable to the first two points but said he wanted a veto power over any licenses of the book since he needed to protect Bill's "exposure." In addition, while he was willing to agree to Steven's having editorial and stylistic control, he wanted his client to have final say over content.

After a few more refinements, we settled on a final contract draft which was eventually signed. By submitting the first contract draft, I was able to ask for certain provisions which I might have been less bold in pressing for prior to the initial agreement. The contract draft permitted me to introduce a number of new goal objectives into the negotiation, based on the firm common ground Steven had established with Bill previously.

5. Delay and Surprise

The moments at which a negotiation occurs and at which the exchange is expected to take place are often critical objectives of one or both of the parties to a negotiation. Using this time factor to advantage can be an effective tactic to substantially influence your opponent's willingness to compromise and concede objectives.

Delay is the tactic of purposely stalling negotiations in the hope that the passage of time will either adversely affect your opponent's bargaining position or cause him to view a particular point at issue in a different light.

A classic example of the effectiveness of delay were the negotiations that brought about an end to the Vietnam war. The North Vietnamese stalled, procrastinated and engaged in a number of other delaying tactics and in so doing, progressively weakened the bargaining position of the United States, which was under mounting pressure from its citizenry to terminate the war.

Delay is useful when the *status quo* works against your opponent's interests, as in the preceding and following situation.

EXAMPLE:

Saul, a California psychologist, contracted to purchase a condominium apartment on the beach in Malibu. Because closing the contract was set to occur just before the summer season, the seller arbitrarily refused to convey title at the agreed-upon date. The seller used the excuse of not being able to find a suitable new apartment to move into as the basis for a request that Saul pay him a $5,000 increase in price to cover his unexpected expenses in having to move into a hotel.

Saul was in a quandary. He desperately wanted to occupy the apartment for the summer and knew that if he took the seller to court, it would take months until the issue was resolved. Reluctantly, he agreed to pay an additional $2,500 if the seller would do what he was already obligated to do—move out then and there.

In Saul's case, the seller had used the tactic of delay in the boldest way possible to renegotiate an increase in price. But delay can also be effective when a negotiation heats up either over a specific point or because of the strain of the circumstances under which the negotiation is occurring. A simple adjournment will permit the parties to cool down, refresh themselves, and re-examine the issues in a more objective light. Often a goal-concession demand that threatens to be a deal-breaker will, with the passage of time, reappear in a less threatening light.

EXAMPLE:

My nephew Michael, age eleven, had been visiting me for two weeks. I invited Chrissy, the daughter of a friend, to spend the weekend as she and Michael had become fast friends.

About an hour she arrived, I heard the pitter-patter of fast-approaching footsteps and tears. It seems that Michael had alluded to the fact that Chrissy was a "lousy skater" and that he would prefer to make his Friday night visit to Skatarama alone. Chrissy was crushed.

Rather than trying to enforce a resolution of the situation immediately, I told them that I felt we should not discuss the matter for at least an hour, but that we would then sit down and work it out. About an hour and a half later, I went upstairs to check on the two of them. Both were in the process of putting on their riding boots, about to head out to the barn. Horses had replaced skates, and the great divide of earlier had all but disappeared.

Use delay whenever it is tactically feasible. But always remember that it can work against you as easily as for you, since it can kill an opponent's interest or otherwise discourage him from pursuing the negotiation. Instead of yielding to the time pressure on him, your opponent may decide to take his losses, terminate the negotiation and pursue the exchange with a more co-operative opponent.

Another tactic that can work for you as easily as it can against you is *surprise*. Surprise involves the introduction into the negotiation of either an unexpected goal objective or a goal objective at an unexpected point in the proceedings. It is sometimes effective because, since your opponent will not have anticipated the objective, he will not have had time to formulate counterrationales or counterbalancing concession requests from you. Consequently, you may be able to win the objective without having to yield anything.

Surprise is frequently used to introduce a primary goal

at the very end of a negotiation in the hope that the weight
of the common ground that has been established by that
time will permit the objective to be won. This often occurs
during a negotiation that is designed to culminate in a contract. Once the negotiation is apparently concluded and one
of the parties takes on the responsibility of drawing up the
contract, he might insert a clause that encompasses a change
in an agreed-upon issue or introduces a new major goal
which he successfully disguised in the negotiation. It is his
hope that the other party's astonishment and resentment
will be ameliorated by the common ground between them
reflected in the contract. Even if his opponent insists on
negotiating the unexpected clause, he is likely to agree to it
in some form.

I am reminded of the experience of an author-client of
mine who was recently approached by a financial investment group with a proposal that he sell all the rights in one
of his published books to a group of investors seeking a tax-
related investment. Beguiled by the money figures that were
thrown at him, he agreed to negotiate. Throughout the negotiation he was told that he would receive $45,000 upon
signing a contract and might receive an additional $280,000
over a period of seven years via the standard nonrecourse
promissory note, if the book was successful. As with all
books, he knew that the likelihood of his getting the
$280,000 or any part of it was remote. But the $45,000 up
front, he was told, was a certainty once he signed a contract
conveying all his ownership of the literary property to the
investment group.

My client agreed and eagerly showed up for the contract
closing. When the contract was laid on the table he immediately noticed that the $45,000 figure he had expected had
been reduced to $15,000. The lawyers for the investment
group gave him all sorts of rationales for this, including their
contention that they had met with difficulties in selling the

book to their investors and were only able to sell it at a markedly reduced figure. My client had only two options, since the contract was presented to him on a take-it-or-leave-it basis. He could walk out. Or he could sign. In view of the fact that he had anticipated receiving some money for his book and, like most writers, needed money, he signed. Of course he insisted afterward that he would "never do business with these people again!" Yet a year later he was back negotiating another such deal.

Had my client in the original instance not needed money, he might well have chosen the option of walking out on the deal. But his opponents had gauged him well and were prepared to take that risk in exchange for the greater likelihood that he would agree to the unexpected reduction in terms.

Surprise can be a treacherous tactic. It can be as destructive sometimes as it is beneficial at others. It should be used sparingly and cautiously, for as often as it may cause an opponent to compromise, it may just as likely cause him to withdraw from the negotiation altogether.

EXAMPLE:

Harris had reached preliminary agreement with Benny to buy his bakery. They had agreed on $75,000 down and promissory notes of $300,000 to be paid off over seven years. Benny had accepted the note concept warily since he didn't want to have to be concerned about the future of the bakery after he sold it. However, he trusted Harris and felt he would be an above-average credit risk.

The transaction was scheduled to be closed at 2:00 P.M. and all parties gathered at Benny's lawyer's office to sign the contracts. Just as they were about to sign the papers, Harris requested a reduction to $25,000 of the cash to be paid on closing the contract, claiming that he had been unable to raise the total amount needed. Benny was totally taken aback. He felt that if Harris had had a problem, he should have spoken with him sooner. As it was, Harris was showing himself to be an unreliable credit risk. Harris' tactic had undermined Benny's whole confidence in the guy. Benny was no longer prepared to proceed with the deal, even on the basis of $75,000 down.

Harris had totally miscalculated the effect his tactic would have on Benny and lost the deal altogether. Had he chosen a different tactic and approached Benny prior to the closing, he probably would have gotten the compromise he was seeking. Both delay and surprise are brinkmanship-like tactics and should be used sparingly, with careful thought given to their relative effectiveness with each differing opponent.

6. "Going Too Far"

It often happens in a negotiation that we will get a signal from our opponent that we are *going too far*. Either we are demanding goal compromises completely out of our opponent's range, or we may not be recognizing one of his essential goals. Conversely, on occasion we will have reason to send out a going-too-far signal to our opponents, a signal that a particular objective is one about which we feel very strongly.

EXAMPLE:

George, a lawyer, had been negotiating a separation agreement on behalf of a male client for some time. His client's estranged wife, Alison, with whom the children lived, did not want to agree to children's visiting rights more often than every two weeks. He had raised the issue three times with Alison's attorney, Aaron, and each time he had been turned down. George's client was adamant in his insistence that he be able to see his children at least weekly and preferably at any reasonable prearranged interval.

George called Aaron and made the strongest pitch he knew how. "Look, Aaron," George said, "my client is unyielding on this point and quite frankly you can't blame the guy. Wouldn't you want the right to see your kid more often than twice a month? I think your position is unreasonable and my client will not accept it. If need be, we'll abort the whole agreement and let the court decide what's reasonable."

George has clearly put out a going-too-far signal. What should Aaron do? What does one do whenever such a signal is received?

In general, so long as the objective is less important to us than to our opponent, we should compromise. But we should use our compromise to get a concession on a more important objective in our favor. When an opponent says that this is an issue which is vital to him, one on which he must achieve some compromise, he is indicating that from his point of view the objective is one about which he would rather terminate the negotiation than concede. But most important, by pinpointing an objective which is so vital to him, the opponent is inviting a demand for a substantial counterbalancing goal concession if you agree to his compromise.

EXAMPLE:

After discussing it with Alison, his client, Aaron decides to concede on the weekly visiting-rights question. However, he intends to make the compromise conditional on George's client's agreeing to his demand for weekly child support of $150, whereas George had previously set $100 as his maximum.

So Aaron calls George and says, "All right, George, weekly visiting rights are okay. But since your client wants to be father of the year, I insist that he make support payments of $150, which you know is not unreasonable. If he truly cares for his kids, he won't mind making the sacrifice."

Aaron has skillfully linked one of his client's most primary objectives to an objective his opponent was forced to admit was absolutely vital to him. Originally, Aaron had thought his client would be lucky to get $125 in support payments, but he now felt confident that because of his compromise response to the going-too-far cry, he'd get his maximum support payment expectation. He does.

Because going-too-far appeals do open up the person making them to the possibility of costly "linked" compromise counterdemands, the appeal is often made and heard through subtle and sometimes even unconscious behavior. People may not consciously realize that they feel that one of their essential interests is being sacrificed, but they will react instinctively. The more obvious sign of such a reaction is withdrawal—in the middle of a negotiation, for no apparent reason, your opponent terminates the negotiation. Or a simple admission of need ("I really can't reduce my price any further") is a form of a going-too-far cry. Almost any plea or behavior which indicates distress should be examined for its underlying cause and purpose. An unrecognized going-too-far signal can destroy a negotiation needlessly. Recognizing it can save the negotiation and possibly give you a unique opportunity to get a major concession in your favor.

Of course, a going-too-far plea can also be nothing more than a bluff, another tactic of negotiation. It is usually pretty easy, however, to expose such a bluff by making the requested compromise but linking it to a major goal objective of yours. If the request is real, a substantial counterbalancing compromise should be forthcoming. If it is not, the plea is probably a bluff and should be resisted.

Finally, when does a going-too-far plea become a useful tactic to use offensively? Usually, only when all else has failed. It's a tactic of last resort. It may well be effective in getting you the particular objective in question, but it may in the end cost you dearly through linked goal concessions. By all means use it rather than give up an absolutely essential objective. But know its potential price.

7.   Bluffs and Diversions

Negotiations thrive on bluffs and diversions. Inherent in almost every negotiating strategy or rationale is a set of assumptions which may or may not be based on reality.

A *bluff* can be defined as a position taken which is not fully supported by fact or logic, but which it is hoped, one's opponent will accept on the assumption that it enjoys such support. The classic milieu of the bluff is the poker table. Poker players will often make a strong bet even though they do not have a strong hand to back it up. The point of the bluff is to persuade the opponent that the player making the bluff has too strong a hand to contest. Bluffing is the art of creating illusions without the use of lies or outright misrepresentations.

EXAMPLE:

Steve Gravely was running for mayor of the small Texas town in which he lived. The incumbent, Rex Renfroe, had been suspected of taking kickbacks and other illegal activities but still had broad support in the town.

Steve's advisers felt that a critical tactic in his campaign to discredit Renfroe would be to challenge him to a series of debates. They did not think Renfroe would accept but they also did not feel Steve would do well if the two actually debated since Renfroe was a powerful speaker.

Steve's offer to debate was a complete bluff. His apparent goal was to set up a debate. His real goal was to show Renfroe's unwillingness to place himself in a position where he might have to answer potentially embarrassing questions.

Steve's tactic worked. Renfroe declined and Steve went on to win the election.

The above example shows a bluff of misdirection, one in which the subject of the bluff is totally illusory and is meant to direct the opponent's attention away from the bluffer's real objective. However in many cases, a bluff is only quantitatively illusory. You may make an offer—for a house, for instance—that represents 70 per cent of your maximum valuation in the hope that your opponent will accept it believing it represents 100 per cent. You may be prepared to complete a particular job in ten days but offer to deliver it in twenty so as to allow yourself maximum flexibility.

The bluff is a fair-game tactic of negotiation because the assumption under which a negotiation usually occurs is that each party need only reveal those goals and that information about them, which the respective party decides or which the parties mutually agree to reveal.

The difference between a bluff and a lie is the difference between illusion and fraud. If your opponent interprets your rationales or goal objectives in a particular way, you are under no obligation to enlighten him differently, provided his interpretation was not caused by your misrepresentation of the facts. In most cases illusion will not occur in those areas that are easily quantified or checked out but rather in the more subjective areas of value, quality and potential.

Naturally, what's good for the goose is good for the gander. If you are entitled to use bluffs in your negotiation, you must expect them to be used against you. Countering your opponent's bluffs is a matter of using half logic and half instinct. The only way for you to smoke out a bluff is by logical deduction and the hope that you will have a smattering of luck to reinforce it. When you suspect a bluff, examine your opponent's goal objectives, his rationales, his alternative proposals. Do they logically support the position he is presenting? Subject him to informational queries and cross-examine his rationales. Do they hold up? Do they show any signs of weakness? How do you feel instinctively?

EXAMPLE:

There was an occasion not too long ago when I was confronted by what smelled to me like a bluff. I was on the verge of selling a manuscript to a hard-cover publisher for a large sum. The publisher was holding out on two final contractual points—the amount of the split between him and the author on any sale of paperback rights and the author's right to approve such a sale. I had asked for a sixty-forty split, 60 per cent to the author and 40 to the publisher, and I was willing to yield on the second point to get it. The publisher was insisting on a fifty-fifty split and would not even consider giving the author paperback-rights sale approval. His rationale for the former was that because of the money and energy he would be putting into the promotion of the hard-cover version of the book its potential paperback value would be greatly enhanced and he should therefore be proportionately rewarded.

The negotiations remained snagged on this issue for several days. I pondered the validity of the publisher's rationale. I even consulted with my client. He sympathized with the publisher's demands and urged me to concede the points since he would be getting a lot of money up front and was anxious to close the deal. I was about to do so when I realized that the money the publisher had agreed to pay for hard-cover rights was considerably more than I had originally expected the manuscript to bring. The publisher had also been a bit too accommodating in acceding to other contractual points which didn't relate to the paperback rights. Was it possible, I wondered, that the publisher had already made a deal with a paperback house for it to buy the paperback rights in the event that the publisher succeeded in getting the hard-cover rights (an increasingly common practice in the publishing industry)? A prior deal would explain his ability to pay such a high advance price for the hard-cover rights. It would also explain his absolute unwillingness to give my client the right to approve the sale of paperback rights. And it would explain the publisher's insistence on a fifty-fifty split. Knowing in advance what the paperback sale would amount to he would want to get as much of it as he could to support his high payment for the hard-cover rights.

I queried the publisher on his rationale for the fifty-fifty split. I phrased my questions in such a way as to indicate my awareness of the possibility that he had already concluded a paperback deal (counterbluff). Eventually I asked him outright if this was true. He was forced to admit it. I should emphasize that I did not feel that he had any obligaion to inform me of his deal in our previous discussions. Had he told me anything else, he would have lied which is completely different from withholding vital information for negotiating purposes.

Subsequently we completed our deal. My client got his sixty-forty split and was willing to give up paperback approval.

Bluffs are fun. They are also serious. By all means use them when it is tactically appropriate. But don't fall into the habit of depending on them, lest you gain a reputation as one who does so. Once you have such a reputation, your negotiating effectiveness will be compromised.

Similar to bluffs are *diversions*, except that diversions are negative bluffs. A diversion is a goal objective that is advanced in a negotiation with little hope of actually securing any concession to it. The sole purpose of diversions is to allow you to accumulate a reserve of goals which can be sacrificed during the negotiation as a trade-off against desired goal concessions by your opponent.

EXAMPLE:

Jason was a part-time actor and had appeared in several plays and films. In reviewing his tax return he noticed that his accountant had deducted all his expenses in going to the theater and movies that year and the cost of an expensive new color television set he had bought.

Jason asked his accountant whether these deductions were allowable. His accountant told Jason that they certainly were since they permitted Jason to keep up with his profession. But he also said that in the event of a tax examination he expected that an IRS auditor would take issue with them. Jason's accountant added that if that occurred he would agree to adjust Jason's tax deduction to 50 per cent of the total expenses. But he wanted to take 100 per cent now so as to have something to "concede" on Jason's behalf if an IRS audit took place.

Jason's accountant had planned a strategy of "quantitative" diversion. His goal was actually to deduct 50 per cent of the total expenses, but he began by deducting 100 per cent so as to be able to compromise part of the deduction with the IRS without going below his minimum objective.

As the above example shows, the tactic of diversion is useful not only in relation to the nature of a particular goal but also in terms of its degree. Price is often deliberately overstated in the sale of real estate, for example, because it is understood that some reduction in price will be negotiated between seller and buyer. The purpose of overstating price is a diversionary one. It is designed to lure a potential buyer into negotiations that will result in concessions on his or her part in exchange for the seller's concession in reducing his or her price demand.

As with bluffs, distinguishing between the real and the unreal—between the essential and the nonessential—is the secret of employing or counteracting the tactic of diversion. When employing diversion, you should use the same technique that you use with a bluff: make it credible—despite the fact that in the end you plan to sacrifice it to gain one or more concessions from your opponent.

The best way to defend yourself against a diversion when it's applied against you is to call your opponent on it, once you are convinced that its only purpose is to serve as a smokescreen. Tell him that you cannot accept the particular objective (diversion) as a serious one on his part. By doing this, if your opponent accepts, even passively, your rejection of it, he will not be able to use it against you later on to counterbalance important concessions you've drawn from him.

EXAMPLE:

I recently purchased a house on which the seller's original asking price was far above its appraised value. The seller was either living in a dream world or using his asking price as a diversion. I challenged him on it immediately and said that I could only begin serious negotiations if he agreed at the outset that the asking price we were talking about was $10,000 less than he had advertised. He replied that he was able to think along those terms and invited me to begin negotiations. Once everything else was out of the way and I had gotten some major concessions from him (move-in date, preclosing repairs, an agreement to install a new well pump, appliances to be included in the purchase price, etc.), he came back with an attempt to restore the original asking price. I laughed and left, my parting shot being that we had already established that the original price was $10,000 more than the agreed-upon basis of our discussions. Two days later he called me (actually, he had his broker call me) to say that he would accept our original deal.

8. *Third-Party Approval Process*

The third-party approval process is characterized by interplay between shields and their principals. You will recall that we discussed this process at some length in Chapter 9, on shields. However, because the third-party approval process can also be used as a valuable offensive tactic, I am including them again here.

You will recall that in certain negotiations your opponent will not be autonomous but a representative of a hierarchy or group, that is, of a third party. Frequently the group will be represented by one of its associates or by an outright shield such as a lawyer or broker. Whatever the case, the representive will have limited authority—real or assumed. You will be told that the group or hierarchy has empowered him to make certain compromises but not others. In the event the negotiation reaches a point at which a compromise or concession beyond the authority of the representative is required, he will tell you that he must refer the concession request to his associates or superiors before agreeing to it, even though he may feel that the concession is warranted.

The third-party tactic will often be used against you for no other reason than to coerce you into reducing your goal objectives or accepting your opponent's. The thinking behind this is that although your negotiating opponent may express his opinion that a particular goal of yours is warranted he is also in a position to advise you that his superiors or associates may not share his opinion. He may be able to convince you that you would be better served by taking a lesser concession within his authority than by letting the issue be removed from the common ground of the one-to-one negotiation. His associates or superiors who are not participants in the actual negotiation, are likely to take a harder and more realistic view of your objectives and reject them, he says. Guessing that you will be reluctant to break the momentum of the negotiation by referring your objectives to people who are not actual parties to the proceedings, your opponent will anticipate that you will accept his reduced proposals. In many cases, he will be right.

The third-party tactic can also be a deterrent to your ambitious goals. Third parties are not subject directly to your rationales, your preparations, or your communications, and it is impossible to convey your rationales or apply your tactics directly to them. They are out of reach and tend to loom in your mind as invisible but omnipotent arbitrary presences.

EXAMPLE:

Sheila was thirty-two and had worked at Howard's department store for two years. She had originally been a sales clerk, but six months ago she was promoted to assistant buyer in the camera department, an extremely profitable part of the store. She had made a number of innovative suggestions which helped boost sales even higher than they customarily were.

Six months is the normal salary-review cycle time for the store, and when the buyer for her department informed Sheila that she was to receive the regular 4 per cent raise, plus a 1 per cent merit increase, she was quite frankly disappointed. She really felt that she deserved more.

She discussed her feelings with the department buyer (and supervisor), who confirmed to Sheila that she was doing an extremely good job and even agreed to increase her merit increase to 1½ per cent, the maximum the buyer was allowed under store policy. Any further increase would have to be referred to the president for approval, and he was known to be tough and to have rescinded, on review, previous department-approved merit increases.

Sheila was in a quandary, but later decided that if she was going to devote her above-average talents to the store's interests, she wanted above-average compensation. She decided, however, to use the boldest tactic possible. Rather than make her request through her department head, she called the president's secretary and asked for an appointment. At the agreed-upon time she went to the president's office and presented her case. The president was so impressed by her initiative (and negotiating ability) that he wanted Sheila to continue in his employ and readily agreed to a 15 per cent merit increase!

Not everyone is a Sheila, and I don't recommend that you all run after your company presidents with demands for giant increases. However, an effective countertactic to be used when dealing with a shield who makes use of his need for third-party approval is to refuse to negotiate with anyone but the person who has the authority to make the final decisions. The alternative is to refuse to recognize the third-party authority and insist that the shield secure his own authority to negotiate within a greater compromise range in advance of your discussions.

In my practice as a literary agent, I usually get authority from my clients to negotiate on their behalf within a certain range. If the negotiation goes beyond that range, I check back with them to get a greater range approved. Of course, I can always say to an opponent, when I need time to consider certain proposals, that I must first check with my client. I usually do check, but in most cases it's a matter of double-checking. In this way I can use the tactic of third-party approval to coerce my opponent or, at least prepare him, to drop or reduce an objective.

Naturally, you will not always be successful in breaking through shields to negotiate directly with the principals. You will often have to endure the third-party approvals process to get any action on your wishes at all, as when dealing with bureaucracies and other institutional organizations. In such cases, you should then formulate your strategy to take the third-party approval process into account, based on what you know of its tactical purposes.

You should also remember that the application of the third-party tactic can be used effectively as an offensive tactic on your own behalf in many situations, and you should not hesitate to do so. You can exploit it either by appointing your own shield to represent and check back with you, or by taking the position that you yourself are a shield and cannot make major decisions without referring the issues to someone else.

How many times have you used the line, "It sounds good to me, but I'll have to check with my wife [husband]?" I have known many people who invent phantom associates to whom they are forever obligated. Here's the story of one fellow who even gave his imagined partner a name and a personality. He talks about the guy all the time, as if he were real!

EXAMPLE:

Harvey was an old-time real estate investor in New York, but this was my first dealing with him. He had called me to make an offer of $150,000 on a property for which I had been asking $225,000.

We bargained back and forth, Harvey having increased his offer to $170,000 and I having reduced my asking price to $190,000. Between each offer, Harvey kept telling me how he felt my asking price was not unrealistic, but that his partner, Burt, was from another era and was very reluctant to increase their offer. At $170,000 versus $190,000, we seemed beyond compromise; $190,000 was my minimum and $170,000 was Harvey and Burt's maximum.

Ten days had elapsed since I last heard from Harvey. Then I received a call from him. Burt was out of town, Harvey told me, and he, Harvey, was prepared to close the deal at $185,000 and explain it to Burt when he returned. Despite having set $190,000 as my minimum, I decided to accept his offer.

When I received the contract of sale from my lawyer, I noticed that only Harvey's name appeared as buyer. I called my lawyer to check whether there had been an error. "What about Burt, Harvey's partner?" I asked.

My lawyer, a veteran in real estate deals laughed and said, "Harvey is Burt, it's his alter ego—Burt only exists in Harvey's mind." Not bad for a phantom, he got me down $5,000 lower than I had intended.

9. The Threat of Withdrawal

The threat of withdrawal is a potentially effective offensive tactic for bringing a stuck negotiation to a successful close. It is best understood by locating it in the context in which it might be used against you. The threat of withdrawal, as well as actual withdrawal, is provoked by one of three things: reassessment, anger, or bluff.

In the case of *reassessment*, what occurs is that one of the parties, perhaps because he is being pressured to concede a goal that is below his minimum objective or because he reviews the negotiation's entire goal-concession package, comes to the conclusion that the total effect of all the goal compromises places him in a position where the exchange is no longer beneficial to him and is possibly even detrimental. He feels that he has negotiated himself into an unsatisfactory outcome. It is very difficult for him at this point to go back and renegotiate the various prior agreements, so he withdraws entirely or threatens to.

Another important contributor in reassessment withdrawal is the fulfillment of certain informational goals at some point in the negotiation that leads your opponent to conclude that the item being exchanged is not what he anticipated. This will probably cause him to withdraw his offer completely or to insist on a complete renegotiation of all the previous goal agreements.

In both cases, if your opponent feels that certain further compromises on your part are warranted, his withdrawal or its threat need not necessarily be taken as final. If you agree that such compromises are reasonable, you will most likely want to suggest an adjustment in previous agreements in order to entice him back to serious negotiations.

EXAMPLE:

A marriage or a situation in which any two people who live together and share a large part of their lives creates a complicated network of objectives and compromises which form the basis of the relationship. The network is usually subject to constant review and can be said to undergo continuous negotiation.

All too frequently, it seems, such a relationship is faced with the threat of withdrawal by one or the other party, and divorce or separation often follows. Of course, in some cases, this is unavoidable and even beneficial. People and circumstances so change as to make the continuation of a relationship counterproductive.

On the other hand, what often happens in a relationship is that a desire develops on one or both parties' part to alter the goal compromises that govern it, rather than an absolute desire to end it. By partners' recognizing that it is the goal agreements governing the relationship that have gone sour and not necessarily love or the desire to be together, many relationships could be saved and a new sense of growth and understanding introduced into them.

A couple I know, both painters, were on the verge of separation. Alice had been the breadwinner in the household for several years, while Bob, without financial success, pursued his art career. After a long time, Alice began to feel that she was unfairly having to sacrifice her ambitions and decided that it was time to pursue her own painting career. She wanted Bob to start assuming economic responsibility for their lives, but felt enormous guilt at forcing him to recognize that he was unable to support them in his chosen work. Alice soon grew to feel deep frustration and anger at Bob and eventually demanded a separation. She failed to see that it wasn't her love for Bob that had waned, but her outlook about their financial roles. Fortunately, Bob refused to accede to her demand. Instead, he engaged her in a series of intense discussions about her feelings and was able to determine the real root of Alice's discontent. He thereupon suggested a new set of financial understandings whereby each would take equal responsibility for their mutual livelihood. Alice was basically agreeable to the new goal compromises, but asked for further assurances such as separate bank accounts and so on.

Today, three years later, Alice and Bob are still together. They are reasonably happy and Alice's painting career has begun to be profitable, as has the art-supply business Bob started shortly after they arrived at their new marital goal compromises. They had the sense to renegotiate their living relationship.

By recognizing that the threat of withdrawal occurs as often out of frustration as it does out of objective thought, the party to a threatened separation would do well to explore carefully the goal compromises under which the threatening party operates and try to discover which goal compromises are no longer acceptable to him or her.

A second reason for withdrawal or its threat is *anger*. The negotiating table is a tense arena. Everyone involved is keyed up to meet the challenge of trading off goal objectives, arguing rationales, and protecting or enlarging their slice of the pie. Tension is as natural to such a setting as high tides are to a full moon. That tension can turn to anger is easy to understand, and the reality is that it often does. There are many reasons for anger to occur. When it does, withdrawal or the threat of withdrawal is often the vehicle chosen to express it.

It is important that anger be vented. Unfortunately, anger often involves a loss of control, a lack of care or forethought about what one bellows. Frequently what one says is: "That's it! I'm fed up! I want no more part of this deal! Find yourself another sucker!" Or something of that sort.

Anger can be costly, however, even when it is warranted and linked to the threat of withdrawal. If your opponent gets *really* angry and threatens to withdraw, your response should be to soothe him and try to effect a reconciliation in order to keep the negotiation going. If you let him leave the negotiating table feeling wronged or unapologized to, he will grow committed to the idea that you have injured him. He will want retribution, which, if the negotiation is resumed later on, may well cost you additional goal concessions if you want to close the deal. These concessions will be equivalent to compensatory damages imposed on you for the supposed insult, rather than concessions resulting from the normal trade-off of goal objectives.

Of course, a clever opponent will never let you know whether his anger is real or calculated. Or if he does, it will be after he has exacted further "guilt" concessions from you and has completed the deal. So be on guard against anger and its accompanying threats. Determine, if you can, whether the anger is real or feigned. And then deal with it accordingly, always aware that whether real or feigned, it is a terrain laden with traps just waiting for you to fall into.

The final reason for withdrawal or its threat resides in the tactics of the *bluff*. From the section on bluffs, above, you can imagine how to deal with such a threat. Question your opponent's previous positions and rationales. Do they logically support his sudden threat of withdrawal at this time? By examining his threat in the light of what has occurred previously, you can easily determine whether you are dealing with a bluff or not. If you determine that you are, then call your opponent's bluff. Most likely he'll back down and resume straightforward negotiations.

It is my experience that most threats of withdrawal are bluffs designed to coerce an opponent into giving in on one or more points. Which is perfectly proper. But most withdrawal bluffs are so transparent as to be immediately ineffective. In the bargain, they seriously erode the bluffer's credibility in the opponent's eye. As a general rule of thumb, you can expect that the longer a negotiation has progressed, the more empty is a threat of withdrawal. Because of this, I would counsel against using the bluff-threat of withdrawal when it comes time for you to engage in offensive tactics.

However, threats of withdrawal based on a reassessment rationale or on carefully directed anger can be very timely.

EXAMPLE:

Jack had tried very hard to please Mrs. Leahy and to comply with each of her requested changes that altered the layout of the new kitchen he was installing for her. All this despite the fact that his contract did not allow for cost overruns and that he knew from experience that Mrs. Leahy would resist paying a dime more than the agreed-upon price. He went along with her because she was an old customer and a source of continuing work.

However, her last request—that he exchange the places where the dishwasher and the sink were going—

would have required him to rebuild half the cabinets he had just made and cause the job to entail a loss for him. Finally, in anger, he told Mrs. Leahy that he was "not going to change another nail and if you don't like it you can pay for my work to date and get another contractor!"

Mrs. Leahy was so surprised by Jack's reaction and the fact that someone had finally stood up to her that she apologized profusely, withdrew her request, and didn't bother him again while he finished the job.

A threat of withdrawal, made in legitimate anger, had gotten Jack what he had found impossible to achieve through compromise.

10.   The Fait Accompli

The *fait accompli*, or "thing accomplished" is a tactic whereby one party unilaterally completes an exchange or presents a goal compromise as accomplished fact and then hopes the other party will agree to it. The expectation is that the objective having been established and embodied in some form as final, or that the event having already taken place, the opponent will therefore accept it with little or no protest.

An example of a *fait accompli* from American history occurred in 1898, when Assistant Secretary of the Navy Theodore Roosevelt ordered Commodore George Dewey to engage the Spanish fleet in the Philippines if (as seemed likely) war broke out between the United States and Spain. Roosevelt did this despite his knowledge of congressional reluctance, should such a war occur, to expand either the conflict beyond Cuba or the United States naval commitment in the Far East. On May 1, about a week after war was declared, Dewey's small fleet arrived in Manila Bay from Hong Kong and within seven hours destroyed or captured the entire Spanish fleet there. Lacking the necessary troops for land operations, Dewey imposed a blockade on Manila Bay. Meanwhile, Roosevelt conveyed his actions after the fact to Congress and requested authorization to send support troops to Dewey. Congress, having little choice, capitulated, and on May 11, General Wesley Merritt, at the head of several thousand troops, was ordered to the Philippines to assist Dewey. On August 14, the United States occupation of the Philippines was completed and officially proclaimed.

But *fait accompli* is not a tactic reserved to high-level political maneuvering. In the following situation, it became an effective tactic to short-cut what might have been a lengthy and futile negotiation between an advertising woman and her former employer.

EXAMPLE:

Barbara, while employed by an advertising agency, had accepted an attractive offer from a rival company to take a job as their head copywriter. As part of the compensation package at her present employers, she was entitled to an annual bonus based on sales with a fixed minimum of $1,000 per year.

Her boss was away on a business trip during the last week of her employment with the old agency, and when she got her last pay check, no proportion of the bonus had been included. Although the bonus was payable at the end of the year she expected to receive at least three months of the bonus at the fixed minimum rate, or $250.

Concerned that her old boss would not pay her what she felt was rightfully hers, Barbara decided to deduct the $250 from the cost of a personal airline ticket she had charged on her company American Express card. The total charge for the ticket was $321, so she sent her old boss a note with a check for $71 explaining her deduction. Her boss never said a word about it and she can only assume he found her deduction valid. Her *fait accompli* had saved Barbara from a lengthy and perhaps unpleasant in-person negotiation.

A *fait accompli* is also useful in the contractual phase of a negotiation. For instance, assume a negotiation has gone back and forth on the provisions to be included in a contract and a final draft has at last been given to you for signature. It accurately reflects all the points you have discussed, but you have thought of another provision you would like added. By adding the provision yourself, signing the contract, and returning it to your opponent without discussing it first, you have carried out a *fait accompli*. You hope that it will be accepted without further negotiation. Provided that it's not a major revision of a previously agreed-upon point or that it doesn't materially alter the terms of the contract, it probably will be.

The risk of a *fait accompli* is that it is a unilateral act which can be challenged *prima facie*, without regard for the merits of whatever it is you have added or subtracted. It places you on the defensive should you be seriously challenged on it. However, the accumulation of common ground embodied in the rest of the exchange has its own momentum, and this will often outweigh most challenges. Despite its risk a *fait accompli* is not only a useful tactic in achieving particular goals but often the only way to break a negotiating deadlock.

11. *The Legal Threat*

The *legal threat* is just what the phrase implies—the threat to take an opponent to court. It is a tactic designed either to start a negotiation or to force a conclusion to an existing but deadlocked one. It usually applies to situations in which a contractual agreement (oral or written) has already been entered into, and one or the other of the parties has then either failed to perform or seeks to renegotiate or modify the terms of the contract. There are occasions, however, when it can be applied prior to the existence of a specific contract.

In the latter instance, the threat of litigation is often used to begin a negotiation. An example of this would be an impending divorce, prior to which one of the spouses refuses to negotiate terms of the financial and property settlement and/or child custody and visitation rights. The threat of litigation—a lawsuit that would require a court to decide the issue—will most of the time coerce the reluctant party into the desired negotiation.

Another example might pertain to an IRS audit. Should you be audited and fail to come to an agreement with the IRS about the outcome, you could use the threat of recourse to tax court to persuade the IRS to arrive at a reasonable settlement.

Lawyers and bill collectors are great proponents of the legal threat, but they tend to overuse it. The expense of both time and money required to carry it out is invariably great, often greater than the monies or other issues involved in the dispute. Frequently lawyers and bill collectors have no intention of going to court to achieve a favorable adjudication of the dispute. Court actions can take months, even years, to be concluded with a commensurate piling up of costs. Yet these practitioners of the lawsuit tactic often employ it to threaten, intimidate, and otherwise coerce their opponents to comply with their demands. And they are often successful because their opponents are either shamed by such reminders of their "bad faith" or are overawed by the prospect of being summoned into court.

By using the tactic yourself, you can frequently achieve the same results. But be sure you know on whom you are using it. Against someone who has a realistic and objective view of the court system it may be useless. In fact, if that someone feels that you have no intention of following up on your threat with actual litigation he may turn it against you, using your reluctance to expend the time and money necessary to resolve your case in court to force you to negotiate greater concessions than you might otherwise be willing to make.

Don't be intimidated by legal threats. This is especially true when you are dunned for past-due bills. If you can't pay them in full, try to turn the legal threat against your opponent. By telling him to go ahead and spend the money and time to take you to court, you can place yourself in a favorable position to negotiate some additional time to meet your obligations.

Whenever it occurs to *you* to use the threat of litigation, always be sure of your position. Such threats are frequently acts of anger or passion. Do not let your emotions rule your objectivity. Make sure that you have an airtight case. And even if you do, do not use the threat unless you are willing to settle for a compromise. If you refuse a compromise and follow your refusal by actually bringing a suit, you may end up with the compromise you were unwilling to accept earlier—by court decree.

EXAMPLE:

Richard recently spent three years in litigation with his ex-wife, whom he had divorced several years earlier. Prior to the beginning of the present legal action, he had received a series of letters from her lawyer demanding a whopping increase in his alimony and child-support payments, which had been set at the time of his divorce. The lawyer's rationale was that Richard was doing much better financially than when he had signed the original agreement and that he should therefore be required to share his increased fortunes with his ex-wife and children. If he didn't, he was informed, his ex-wife would take him to court.

Richard consulted a lawyer and learned that unlike most other contracts, a divorce agreement could always be changed by a court, particularly when child support was involved. He was agreeable to a modest increase in his payments—one that would be in fair proportion to his increase in income. But he refused to agree to the amount demanded by his ex-wife, which he felt would leave him financially strapped and unable to make a go of his second marriage. He offered a well-reasoned compromise settlement. She refused and instituted proceedings to get the amount she wanted.

The court action dragged on for three years, punctuated by periodic reoffers by Richard of his proposed compromise settlement, one that he remained convinced was fair. His ex-wife consistently refused to entertain ideas of settlement and pressed her cause with increasing fervor and hostility in court. After a great deal of acrimonious testimony was heard, the court made its decision. It awarded the ex-wife almost exactly what Richard had offered to pay her three years earlier. Of course, by dragging him into court the woman forced him to incur $10,000 in legal fees for his defense—an expense he could well have done without. Then her lawyer produced a bill of $12,500 for representing her—an expense, given her courtroom representations of herself as being on the edge of poverty, she surely could have done without. All for the sake of an approximately $50-per-month increase in her ex-husband's payments.

The old saying has it that the only winners in a litigation are the lawyers. As a tactic, the threat of litigation can
be effective if applied in timely and judicious ways. The actuality of litigation, however, can be a costly one. In the example above, the ex-wife could have asked for more than
she was getting, and gotten it, simply through the threat of
litigation. But, whether out of greed or vindictiveness or
both, she chose to "ask for everything and get it" through
actual litigation. Unless her lawyer forgave her $12,500 in
fees (which was highly unlikely), she ended up getting less
than she would have in the first place.

12. Take-It-or-Leave-It Positions

The purpose of a *take-it-or-leave-it position* is to let
your opponent know that this is your best offer, that it represents the maximum in goal compromises you are prepared
to make. Its advantage is fairly obvious. By declaring it a
take-it-or-leave-it offer, you have pre-empted your opponent's ability to test your willingness to make further compromises. He must either accept your offer or else reject it,
knowing that there will be no further offers.

EXAMPLE:

Tim had been after his father to play tennis with
him for the last three weekends. Finally, Tim's father
promised to play, but told Tim that they would only be
able to play for an hour that afternoon since he had to
pick up a friend at the four-o'clock train.

Tim protested. He wanted to play for at least an
hour and a half and didn't want to play this afternoon
since he was hoping to watch his favorite football team
in the playoffs.

His father replied by saying that it was up to him,
but the only time he could foresee being able to play in

the near future was that afternoon for an hour. His father structured a take-it-or-leave-it position. Tim took it.

In making a take-it-or-leave-it offer, you theoretically take the risk that your offer will be rejected and you will not have a chance to improve it. In reality, of course, nothing stops you from making a new offer once your take-it-or-leave-it offer has been rejected. You will lose a certain amount of bargaining credibility, but this is an acceptable risk, particularly if you place your revised offer in the context of some sort of face saving.

EXAMPLE:
Assume that Tim had declined his father's invitation and decided to watch the playoffs instead.
Later that afternoon Tim's father says to him, "Look if we get up extra early, I can sneak an hour and a half of tennis in tomorrow morning. How about it?"

The logic behind a take-it-or-leave-it strategy is that your opponent will agree to a lower mix of goal compromises if they are presented as a final offer than if they are presented so as to give him the opportunity of negotiating each one. Of course, the absence of negotiation also places you in the position of not being able to determine through the give-and-take of rationales exactly what your opponent's minimum goal expectations are. It is quite possible that by establishing a take-it-or-leave-it position, you may offer more than your opponent's minimum expectations.

EXAMPLE:
Clark headed a management negotiating team which was meeting in twelve-hour shifts with union representatives in an effort to avoid a strike. All issues

had been settled except wage increases and the number of vacation and sick-leave days.

The union representatives had asked for a minimum increase of 32 per cent in wages over three years (16 per cent the first year, 8 per cent each for the second and third years). In addition, they wanted three-week vacations for all employees, plus up to ten days of sick leave to be added to vacation time if not taken as sick days.

Clark had made various compromise suggestions, including wage increases totaling 22 per cent and three weeks vacations for all employees after four years' employment and seven days of sick leave without the add-on feature.

Time was running short, and Clark knew that if negotiations continued at their present pace, the two parties would never resolve the few remaining major items. He decided to use a take-it-or-leave-it tactic.

He explained his time concern to the union negotiating team and said he would make his best take-it-or-leave-it prestrike offer. A 27 per cent increase in wages spread equally over three years, three-week vacations for four-year employees, and seven days of sick leave with the add-on feature.

The union representatives asked for a short recess to consider the offer. The union's previously determined minimum wage goal was 25 per cent. They were delighted with the offer and readily accepted it.

The take-it-or-leave-it tactic is most often used when a negotiation has proceeded for a while and becomes stuck on one or two critical issues. By structuring a final and enforced compromise, an opponent's resistance can sometimes be jolted into acceptance.

When on the receiving end of a take-it-or-leave-it offer,

although it contradicts the apparent basis on which the offer was made, it is usually possible to counteroffer with at least one or two modifications. In the worst case, your opponent will reject the modifications and remind you that the offer was "nonnegotiable" and final. However, it is more likely that he will take your requests under consideration.

EXAMPLE:

Bob had received a final offer on his house of $65,500. He had begun by asking $72,500, and the buyer's first offer was $60,000. Bob had come down to $67,000 and the buyer had come up to $64,000.

Bob was more or less ready to accept the buyer's so-called "final offer," but decided he would first attempt one more go at a $500 increment. He countered with $66,000. The buyer mumbled that his offer of $65,500 was meant as his final offer. But he liked the house too much to lose it for $500. That and the fact that he and Bob had established so much common ground caused him to accept Bob's counteroffer.

Chapter 13

How the Experts Do It

In the course of writing this book, I decided that it would be useful to test my theories against the experience and knowledge of a number of people who have built distinguished professional careers as a result of their skill in negotiation. What I wanted to learn, basically, was what they did differently than I when applying negotiating strategies to the ordinary and extraordinary transactions of life. To the extent they did, I wanted you to know about it. What I found was that, either instinctively or consciously, all follow in their own ways more or less the prescriptions I have set out in these pages.

Theodore Kheel, for instance, is a New York attorney who is known to anyone in that city who reads a newspaper. Almost any time a major labor crisis or some other form of municipal unrest occurs, Ted Kheel is called in by the incumbent mayor and union leaders to mediate and bring about a settlement satisfactory to all parties. In many ways he has at times exercised more influence over the city than any of its mayors during the past twenty years.

How does he do it? Primarily by practicing the techniques which I have outlined in the foregoing chapters. First of all, he prepares. "You've got to know what's occurred in the past with respect to each party," he says, "how and why they have chosen to take the positions they have. Second you have to create for yourself a distance from the issues. Not remoteness or indifference. But an 'interested disinterestedness.' Third, you've got to test your parties to see what's absolute and unyielding in their demands and what's pliable and flexible. And of course you've got to know your people. You have to know how much they know—how much is pragmatic, realistic knowledge, how much is grandiose wish, and how much is some kind of ego pursuit. Once you have these four factors in hand, you then begin to apply specific strategies and techniques."

Kheel is speaking mainly about his role as a mediator, as one who orchestrates a negotiation between two opposing parties. But, he says, "the same rules apply when I am negotiating on my own behalf. Information and preparation—you would be surprised how effective these factors alone can be in getting what you want. Indeed, they in themselves can be a useful tactic and can obviate the need to engage in more specific tactics. By being able to let your counterpart know that you have a lot more accurate information about the object of the transaction than he expects you to have, you can block him from engaging in a lot of tactics and ploys of his own. He's likely to say, 'Oh, well, there's no fooling this guy, might as well get on with it and get it over with.'"

What's the best way to get a negotiation started, even when the other party has no desire to enter into an exchange? "The next time you read in the papers about Company X trying to take over Company Y," Kheel replies, "observe the amount of information gathering and preparation

Company X engaged in before making its intentions known. Company Y doesn't want to enter into a merger or takeover transaction. But when confronted with Company X's preparation, it often has little choice. Now this is often coercion, and there is something clearly deceptive about it, even though it is permitted by law. I'm not saying that your readers should engage in deception or coercion. I make the point to illustrate my thesis that preparation and information on the part of one party will often succeed in getting the other to negotiate a deal.

"It's not just a matter of acquiring knowledge," he goes on, "but of effectively imparting it to your opponent. The most graphic example of this is in the criminal-law system. Say you're a district attorney and you've got a guy who's clearly committed a crime. You get an indictment and bring the guy to trial. The guy is guilty as all get out. He knows it and knows that you know it and that you have a decent chance of proving it beyond a reasonable doubt. But there's no way he's going to plead guilty. You can inform him of the consequences to him if and when he's found guilty by the jury. If he's convinced, you can then offer to negotiate a series of lesser consequences in exchange for him pleading guilty to a lesser charge. You do this because you want to avoid a long expensive trial, you want to avoid the remote chance that the jury will let him off and you want to get the guy off the streets. Once he's persuaded of the greater consequences to him, he'll be willing to negotiate the opportunity to suffer the lesser ones."

I asked Kheel for an example of a real-life negotiation of his in which knowledge and preparation conquered all. He recalled a strike-settlement negotiation between all of New York's newspapers and one of the unions that had struck them. "It was eventually resolved on the simplest of developments, and it was the application of some plain, hard-nosed knowledge that did it. The union was holding out for all sorts of stiff demands with respect to complicated wage increases, vacation time, work conditions, health benefits, and a dozen other things which, if granted, would knock a few of the papers out of business. I pointed out to the union president that if the strike lasted much longer, several of the papers would go out of business anyway. This would throw almost half his membership out of work. Since the affected papers were old New York standbys, most of the men thrown out of work would be those who had elected and supported him a number of years before. There was a 'Young Turk' faction in the local that had been trying to get rid of him for some time. The faction was made up mostly of workers who worked on the more financially stable papers that were not threatened with bankruptcy by the strike. If the strike went on much longer and the older papers were forced to fold up, I told the union leader he would lose much of his constituency. With his principal supporters out of work, they were likely to abandon their support of him and open the way for the Young Turks to vote him out of the presidency of the local at the next election. He quickly saw the light, modified the union's demands, and brought an almost instant end to the strike."

Geraldine Stutz is another well-known New Yorker. As the chief executive of Henri Bendel, perhaps the city's leading specialty store for women, she has put her stamp on the retail clothing industry as an arbiter of taste and originator of fashions. She has reached the pinnacle of her profession through exceedingly skillful business management. In her view, the key to successful business management and leadership is negotiation. "It is persuading people to do what they don't always want to do and to enjoy it in the bargain," she says.

Ms. Stutz runs a business that demands a large staff of

sales people, buyers, clerks, bookkeepers, maintenance people, and so on. She also must deal intensively with other businesses—designers and manufacturers who supply her store with its varied merchandise, distributors, shippers, and other support organizations. How does she successfully juggle all these duties in terms of direct negotiation?

"In the first place," she says, "I operate at an advantage, and that is the Henri Bendel name. I am enormously proud of what the name represents and I base every negotiation or transaction I engage in on maintaining its symbol of quality. I simply and absolutely refuse to engage in anything that has the remotest chance of sullying the name, and most people with whom I do business are aware of that. Which saves a lot of wasted time in negotiation."

Ms. Stutz names style as a major ingredient in effective negotiating. "Of course," she says, "you've got to know what you're doing. You've got to know all the issues and nuances and consequences involved in the deal, and you have to know how to properly integrate them. This is part of getting your information and making your preparations. But to me, the most effective negotiator is the one who, having prepared himself on the issues involved, is capable of making the deal seem attractive to the other side merely through the use of his style of doing business. Sure, style can fool you. I mean I have negotiated with real smoothies who seemed a pleasure to do business with, only to find later that they lied or made false commitments. But that's not the style I'm talking about. To me, good negotiating style is calmness and sincerity as you lay out your position, and inviting the other party to do the same thing. This fosters a spirit of co-operation and trust. Once that is established, it is much easier to work out the issues. Also, it's easier to be more stubborn when you are calm and sincere. And you can always be a bit mysterious, too. In other words, keep your opposite number thinking about you. The more he thinks about you, the less he is likely to be locked into his own demands. On the other hand, sometimes I make an effort to have the person I'm dealing with know something about me —something that accords with his own interests in life. I encourage the other person to do the same. In some negotiating situations, when the parties know something about each other personally it is often easier to understand each other's goals. It is easier to explain why you can't agree to this or that but might be interested in an alternative. That to me is one of the keys to concluding a negotiation successfully. It's knowing the person you're negotiating with, knowing his likes, dislikes, idiosyncrasies, and so on. Getting a feel for his personality and character. These things can tell you so much. The ultimate object of the negotiation becomes not the issues, nor the items, nor the money, but the person. If you sell the person on yourself, you can usually end up getting what you want."

Felix Rohatyn has functioned for many years as a partner in one of Wall Street's most eminent financial institutions, Lazard Frères. More recently he has become known to the general public as the head of the Municipal Assistance Corporation, the organization set up by the State of New York to help New York City recover from its financial woes. Rohatyn has long been a legendary negotiator in the rarefied atmosphere of high finance and big business. It was for his understanding of finance and his financial negotiating skills that he was selected to run "Big Mac," as the Municipal Assistance Corporation was dubbed shortly after its creation in 1976, when New York City teetered on the brink of bankruptcy.

I asked the busy Rohatyn to outline his negotiating principles. Information, preparation, and the establishment of a flexible strategy were all items he mentioned as being

absolutely necessary. "No one can hope to negotiate successfully purely on 'charm'," he said. "The more you know about
the problems and the better prepared you are to deal knowl-
edgeably with unexpected twists and turns, the better off
you are."

But assuming that both parties are fully and equally informed and are equipped with equally sound strategies,
what is it that enables one of them to come out ahead so
much more often than the other? "That's where the real skill
comes in," Rohatyn said. "I suppose it's an intangible, hard
to define with any exactitude. The closest you can come to
defining it is to say that the person best able to establish and
sustain the spirit and tenor of a negotiation is the one who
most often is the winner. It's not a gift of talk or anything
like that. It is simply a question of remaining in control of
the proceedings. The best way to do that is to impart to the
opposite party the feeling that the negotiation in question is
of extreme importance and that you are quite serious and
genuine in your pursuit of it."

When asked to be more specific, Rohatyn said, "There
are many ways to do this. First, you let the opposite party
see the extent to which you have informed yourself and
have prepared. That convinces him of the seriousness and
importance, to you at least, of the business at hand. And
then you go on to do other things to further establish in his
mind your sincerity, credibility, and good faith. Once the
other party is convinced of these things, he will more likely
than not try to accommodate you. Which is not to say that
he'll automatically yield to all your needs and desires. But
he will approach the deal with the same intensity that you
do. You've got to make it as important to him as he thinks it
is to you. That is the secret of good salesmanship, which is
what negotiation is all about. The most successful salesmen
are not those who depend on flattery, cajolery, glibness, and
so on. They are those who make the deal important—not

only to themselves but to their customers. And in my experience the one who does this best is the one who takes the low-key approach. Low-key but urgent. That is how I negotiate. It is the best way to shape and control the direction of a negotiation. Tactics are fine, but they are useless unless you are in control of them. If you are well prepared and can manage the pace and intensity of the negotiation, you will remain confident. Your confidence will make an impression on the other person, and he will seek to match it. The best tactic is confidence. A cool attitude toward the issues and a warm one toward the person with whom you are negotiating."

Marvin Miller is the head of the Major League Baseball Players' Association, a kind of quasi union of professional ball players. Miller is celebrated in the sports world as the man who revolutionized baseball salaries by forcing teams to compete for the services of players rather than, as was the tradition, owning those services in perpetuity. Previously a ball player, once he signed a contract with a team, was somewhat of an indentured servant—albeit a nicely paid one. He could be sold, traded, demoted, or retired at the whim of the team's management, without having any say in the matter. Miller challenged this system in the courts and won, establishing the principle of the free agent. Thereafter, a ball player was beholden to his team for only a year beyond the expiration of his yearly contract, after which he could offer his services on his own to any other team that might be interested in bidding for them.

I asked Miller about his negotiating principles. He suffers a mildly unfavorable reputation in the sporting press as a man who negotiates by ultimatum. In a sense this is true, but only because he has a powerful group behind him. Its power lies in the fact that if its membership votes to

strike, as it did a few years ago, the owners and management of the Big League teams cannot earn any income.
Since most major league baseball franchises have little in
the way of capital surpluses, they need the ongoing reve-
nues from game attendance to stay in business.

Miller cautions against negotiating by ultimatum in
most circumstances, however. All he tries to do, he says, is to
enlighten his opponents to the realities of the deals he seeks.
In ordinary negotiations, his first principle is to engage his
opposite number in a mutual declaration of maximum demands and then work from there. In other words, he immediately puts all his, or his client's, maximum goals on the
table and asks his opponent to do the same with respect to
his. Since he, like any good negotiator, believes that everything is negotiable, he establishes the stiffest terms he can
and expects his opposite number in the negotiation to do the
same. Once the issues are joined, he then proceeds to negotiate on a term-by-term basis. He has little use for shilly-
shallying, ploys or small talk. He is all business and feels
that his imperial, businesslike approach is the best and most
expeditious way to get the desired results. He cares little
about knowing his opponent and endorses the idea that the
issues themselves shape the tenor and substance of a negotiation. One thing that is immediately noticeable to anyone
who negotiates with him is his refusal to be intimidated into
making concessions because of extraneous factors, such as
the celebrity or social standing of an opponent. By concen-
trating on the issues, he says, he is able to put extraneous
matters out of mind.

Such things as tactics and techniques are buried in the
issues, he believes. Once the issues are joined, a negotiating
dynamic emerges which, in his view, has a life of its own.
He believes in letting the issues do the work and says that
all he does essentially is to guide the negotiation, much as

an automobile driver does his car, under the power of the dynamo of issues.

You will gather from the foregoing that every expert negotiator has his or her pet approaches. I could quote a number of others with whom I talked, but I believe I have made my point. There is no single magic formula for negotiating success. There are as many ways to negotiate as there are people who negotiate. Some place the most emphasis on knowledge and preparation, others on style, others on the issues and terms, others on personal interaction. Understandably, none of those I spoke with was willing to reveal specific tactics and techniques they employ. But all agreed that tactics are effective only insofar as they are supported by solid information and preparation. And all likewise concurred in my contention that controlling the tenor of a negotiation is probably the most important facet of the negotiator's art. All are thoroughly experienced at this and accomplish it most times as a matter of second nature. What they do, in effect, is engage in negotiation at its highest and most sophisticated level, which is the subject of my next and final chapter.

Chapter 14

Playing the Inner Game

In 1974 a best-selling book was published by Random House called *The Inner Game of Tennis*. In it the author, W. Timothy Gallwey, presented a new theory for the game of tennis and, by extension, for many other competitive activities. The theory was that no matter how expert a player is in strategy, tactics, and techniques, and no matter how intensely his competitive flame burns, it is his ability to play the "inner game" that will be the measure of his consistent success. In its oversimplified outline, the inner game of tennis is the competition that occurs within each person as he tries to meet the challenge of whatever outer game he's involved in. It is combination of concentration, confidence, and relaxation. These three qualities, when they cannot be sustained throughout the course of a match, are usually the underlying reason for defeat. They cause a technically superior player to play below the level of his ability. Likewise, when they are sustained by an inferior player, they cause him to play at a level that is considerably above his natural ability. By learning how to excel consistently at the inner game of tennis, the author claims, any player will improve his outer game immeasurably. By mastering the inner game, one masters oneself and is therefore able to shape and control the tenor and rhythm of the match.

Every negotiation has a distinct tenor and rhythm. The ultimate tactic of the negotiator is to shape and control the negotiation by shaping and controlling its tenor and rhythm. This is best achieved by mastering what I, borrowing from the tennis analogy, will call the *inner game of negotiation.*

The basic elements of the inner game of negotiation are simply, as they are in tennis, concentration, confidence, and relaxation. Every time you enter a negotiation it will begin to take a shape created partly by its tenor—amiability, hostility, indifference—and partly by its pace or rhythm— hurried, leisurely, high-pressured, low-pressured. Much of the tenor and rhythm will be dictated by the interplay of attitudes and style between you and your opponent. Will he indulge in numerous bluffs, diversions, or other tactics? Will the negotiation be based on mutual respect or will it be one of mismatched adversaries? Is your opponent's desire to reach a "fair" deal for both parties, or is it to get everything he can with no consideration at all for your needs and goals?

Frequently in a negotiation, an opponent will be intimidating simply by the force of his or her personality or station in life. At the other extreme, he might be apparently meek and sympathy-seeking. Or he might be overly friendly or intimate. He could be diffident, revealing nothing of his reactions. Or he might be enthusiastic.

No matter what the case, your opponent will try to impose his own tenor and rhythm at the start. Through them he will seek to control the negotiation and put you on the defensive—whether by means of kindness, rudeness, or indifference. Your task is to ignore your opponent and concentrate on the issues themselves. It is the issues that are the determining factors of the negotiation, not your opponent. If you are able to do this, you will shape the tenor and rhythm to your purposes, and whatever strategy and tactics you use will have that much more effect.

Sounds good, but how to do it? I refer you back to the concept of the inner game. While you are competing with your opponent in a negotiation, you are also competing with yourself. You are competing with your own weaknesses, which you know far better than your opponent ever can. If your opponent is shrewd, he will probe for those weaknesses. If you are adept at the inner game, he will never find them and will have to return his focus to the issues.

In the inner game of tennis, you do not play your opponent so much as you play the ball. The ball is your prime opponent, and the ball as it relates to you is the inner game. You concentrate on the ball, on the act of stroking it across the net, on the mechanics of the act. You form a concentrated image in your mind's eye of the entire action and its desired outcome. Then you try to impose the image you have created upon the reality or actuality of stroking the ball.

The inner game of negotiation works in much the same way. You concentrate on the points at issue in the negotiation—the back-and-forth of goals, tactics, and concessions. You form pictures in your mind of the tactics and techniques you wish to apply to the issues. Then you convert those pictures to the reality of applying the tactics and techniques. Let your opponent carry on in whatever fashion he prefers. Your opponent is not the issue. His goals are, relative to yours.

As you learn to concentrate exclusively on the issues and positions, you will gain both confidence and relaxation, the two other vital factors of the inner game. You will grow confident in your ability to co-ordinate tactics with issues, and as you do that, you will acquire the relaxed manner necessary for you to control the rhythm and tenor of the negotiation. In your control, the rhythm and tenor will be invaluable in creating an atmosphere in which the optimum mix of goal concessions is possible.

By becoming adept at the inner game of negotiation, you will possess all that you'll require to negotiate effectively with anyone about anything. Your inner game-derived manner and style will convince people to enter into negotiations with you by forcing them to deal with you and your proposals on a serious and respectful basis and may well elicit from them the concessions and compromises you need to conclude favorable agreements.

The inner game is the most subtle of all negotiating tactics, but the most vital. It is so vital that you should think of it not just as a tactic but as an entire negotiating style and posture. Its mastery requires practice and experience.

Finally, I would like to share with you the ultimate wisdom of all life's inner games as I have come to know it. That wisdom, in a word, is *perspective*. Perspective is the vital force that can invalidate any power, any intimidation, any attempt at control or domination of our inner selves by another person or persons.

The wisdom of perspective is placing the moment, event, or person that is threatening to dominate us in the correct perspective of time, of our society, indeed, of the history of civilization.

We tend to think of things only in so far as they relate to the moment and context in which they occur. The importance and significance of an event is inversely proportionate to time and space. A missed airline connection causing a five-hour delay can seem intolerable at the moment it occurs. However, if you look back on it in the context of a three-week trip, it loses almost all of its hardship and significance.

I recently headed off from my New York office for my regular weekend train journey to the country. I arrived at Grand Central Station to discover that I had had a lapse, that the train I thought left at 8:30 P.M. had actually left at 8:15. It and the woman I live with had left without me. My first reaction was rage at myself, the world, the trainmaster, everything. Then I said to myself, "Don't be stupid. What's a missed train in a lifetime in the history of the world? Forget it—it's not the last train you'll miss." There were no more trains that night to the town where I was going, so I took a train to a town forty miles away and then had a cab drive me home. A little creative rerouting and $50 had saved me from a night of self-anguish.

The lesson of perspective can be equally applied to the negotiating process and be invaluable in seeing the true cost or benefit of a particular goal compromise or exchange. All too often, in the heat and moment of a negotiation, we come to overestimate the value of a particular goal objective or even the exchange itself. This can cause us to make serious errors in judgment, either as to whether to concede a particular goal compromise or, alternatively, as to whether to walk away from the negotiation and perhaps give up the exchange altogether.

In order to gain perspective in this or any situation, stop and ask yourself the perspective question. Set the item in doubt in a future time reference and context. What will the realistic cost to me a year from now be of my granting this goal compromise? (I have seen million-dollar real estate negotiations collapse over a $500 adjustment item.) How would I feel about this issue if I were on the beach of a Caribbean island? If I walk out of the negotiation today and forego the exchange, how will I feel about its loss six months from now? How will the compromise in question make me feel tomorrow, next month, five years from now? Will it contribute or detract from my well-being and happiness now and in the future?

Life is a game, particularly modern life. Once the stakes go beyond food and shelter, the rules become arbitrary, the wins and losses self-determined. Keep the game in perspective and you'll be a sure winner at the inner game. Win the inner game and you can't lose at the outer.